HONOURING
YOUR TRUE SELF

HONOURING
YOUR TRUE SELF

EVIE FLYNN

First published 2019

© 2019 Evie Flynn

Illustration by Ciara Flynn
Typeset and designed by Karl Hunt

ISBN: 978-1-6979037-4-4 (pbk)

CONTENTS

PREFACE

We live in a time of shifting sands regarding relationships, identity, gender, and social norms. As the sands shift, there has never been a time when connection to our true self has been more important. Connection requires an honesty, humility, and trust that allow us to step into our vulnerability. This is a necessary part of acknowledging who we are so that we can allow others to truly see us. It is from this place that the inexplicable mystery of intimacy can unfold and a *true-self-to-true-self* connection with another can emerge and grow.

At the heart of this book is the belief that our first belonging must be to our self, this means building and nurturing a compassionate relationship internally first. Too often, we give authority to parts of us that self-doubt, criticize and limit us to a narrow version of who we are and we turn away from our inner wisdom and inherent value. The work of this book is to highlight the process of building a conscious, deliberate, intentional relationship with our true self first and foremost, and then with others. Its focus is on developing the nurturing experience that such a relationship can become, so that we can really honour ourselves and in doing so, we shift out of the straight jacket that we pulled on as younger people. By lifting the lid on our relationship patterns, we shine a light on the beliefs about ourselves that we constructed at an earlier time when we were young and more impressionable, and had no other experience or context with which to understand or view others.

Therefore, this book places huge emphasis on learning to really trust ourselves. It encourages us to break free from the reactive behaviours that subconsciously become such a huge part of our relationships. As long as we continue with these automatic responses, we repeat the same patterns over and over again each time we enter a relationship.

The writing of this book has paralleled my own pathway into deepening my relationships. It has been a very significant part in my journey to becoming a psychotherapist where I can now be present and open to meeting each new mysterious and meaningful experience as it emerges and unfolds, in the relationship with myself and with others. By learning to turn in a compassionate way towards myself, I can create a space where very meaningful parts that I had disconnected from and continued to run from, can now be acknowledged, held, nurtured and integrated. As a result, I can now experience my relationships in a hugely meaningful way where feelings of trust and belonging can replace fear and uncertainty.

Like all beginners, I began my journey by taking small steps. However, as I learned to express myself in a whole-hearted and honest way in my relationships, I realised that my worries about how I would be perceived when I connected with my humility, vulnerability and imperfect humanity, were unfounded. Instead, I discovered the most unexpected moments of intimacy. Most profound has been my ability to experience feelings of love, self-worth, and belonging, as increasingly I allow myself to be truly seen, and from this new place of heart connection where I now reside, I can truly see others.

This book is intended to be a companion on your journey towards building a conscious relationship with yourself, and then in the space you create with others. It provides a psychological map of how the relationship sphere opens up our vulnerability. In our fast-paced society, we are pulled externally for validation, for approval, for value, and self-esteem. Suddenly, we are supposed to be proficient in all these different realms in our lives. I believe that we need to come back to base where we construct a compassionate relationship with all parts of our self, including our imperfect parts. We develop a meaningful connection with this self from a place of inner presence and heartfelt connection. From this place we can meet the world and its many demands with steadiness and strength.

INTRODUCTION

Almost 41% of marriages in America end in divorce, with one in two marriages ending in separation. In the UK, this figure is almost identical, with a divorce rate of 42%. Failure is not bad; it is just the devastating consequences that result from the severing of a union that sprang from such huge hope.

If you are reading this, you have probably reached a point in your life where you are questioning yourself or a relationship. It may have taken an unexpected turn and you are looking for answers or the courage to take a step in a new direction, or something unexpected may have happened and you are experiencing feelings of rejection, abandonment, frustration, or hurt.

I want to help you turn that around and bring you to a place where your aspirations and desires can be explored and fulfilled in a meaningful and integral way, where you can hold your feelings of disappointment and grief in a compassionate space without identifying with them, and you place yourself in a position of value and regard in your relationships.

I reached a point in my life when I got really tired of making the same mistakes over and over again. I realised that something had to change. I no longer wanted to rely on others for acceptance and fulfilment. Deep down I knew I needed to take back control. What I did not realise was the enormity of the potential that would open up to me when I made this decision.

My journey was triggered by something that no human journey can be experienced without: heartbreak. It is the greatest crucible for growth. When we open up that most tender part of ourselves to somebody else, only for it to get crushed and broken, the resulting feelings of grief and betrayal can be paralysing. Heartbreak has had the single most powerful effect on my life; nothing else has forced me to confront myself the way it has. It was only when I was faced with the consequences of such devastating anguish, that I was presented with an opportunity to look into myself and explore what led me to this place of suffering. For the first time in my life I wanted to take responsibility for my actions. I needed to find out what were the thoughts, beliefs and behavioural patterns that yielded such a disappointing result for me in my relationship, and how could I turn this around?

In an effort to demystify questions about my own relationship, I embarked on a pathway that led me to study psychotherapy. There, I discovered a whole new world of meaning and intelligence about relationships. I became intrigued by the psychology that lies at the very core of how we connect with and relate to others. This realisation heralded the beginning of a huge journey of self-growth where I could understand the misinformed beliefs I had about myself (and who I needed to be) in order to be regarded. By confronting my behaviour in an honest and compassionate way, I was able to uncover the mystery behind why I found myself in a continuous cycle that began with excitement and hope but ended in disappointment, frustration, and isolation. As a result, the feelings of trust and regard that I now experience in my relationships mean that I no longer second-guess myself. Instead I can belong first and foremost to myself and then to a relationship where I am seen and valued.

I want to support you on a journey to reaching fulfilment and meaning in your relationships. In particular, I will provide insights into the emotional and psychological shifts that occur in romantic relationships and support you in creating meaningful connections where you can remain steady and grounded and at the same time allow intimacy to develop and grow.

CHAPTER 1

UNDERSTANDING RELATIONSHIPS

To the degree that we look clearly and compassionately at ourselves, we feel confident and fearless about looking into someone else's eyes.

Pema Chödrön

The renowned psychiatrist Dr. Daniel Siegel[1] defines relationships as "the sharing of energy and information. We can do it with people, and nature." We are relational beings with a strong need for love and belonging. In fact, our basic psychological need is to love, to be loved, and to belong to something

1   Siegel, D. J. [2008]. The Neurobiology Of We: How relationships, the mind, and the brain interact to shape who we are, Sounds True Inc

greater than ourselves. Without relationships we would not have a system to regulate ourselves. As a trained ecologist, I learned that one of the most fundamental laws of nature is that the level of cohesion and integrity that exists within any relationship determines its ability to survive. This survival strategy, which is present in all natural habitats, is the same in human relationships. We are continuously adapting to what helps us to survive and this includes forming supportive relationships with others. The quality of our relationships has a direct impact on our quality of life. We feel a sense of belonging when we are part of a connection that is meaningful. It is these very significant needs for connection and belonging that beckon us to take huge risks and invest in relationships to new and uncertain destinations. However, as a relationship continues, we very often encounter unexpected and unfathomable changes in the space we share with our partner. I became very curious about this shifting landscape and how we respond to it. In particular, I wanted to explore how we can stay true to ourselves so that we can honour our desires while at the same time, we remain open to maintaining a true connection. I discovered that key to achieving this within a relationship is the quality of the connection we develop and nurture with ourselves. As Pema Chödrön maintains, when we can act from a place of self-seeing and self-compassion, our relationships stem from an inner connection with ourselves. It is this inner connection that influences the quality of the connections we share with others. When this internal space includes feelings of understanding and tenderness, we can allow ourselves to be truly seen. From this place, we can truly see others. It is through consciously and purposefully recognising and inviting our internal emotional experience and responding compassionately to it, that we bring about the greatest shift in how we shape our relationships with others. Staying in the present moment enables us to recognise, acknowledge, and respond to our emotions and feelings as they arise. This significantly influences our ability to live a fulfilling and meaningful life.

Conversely, when we do not remain compassionate, conscious, and present in our relationships, we cannot respond in any meaningful way or develop true connections with others. Instead, we act from an unconscious script that was constructed at a much earlier time.

Our script is made up of the belief systems, decisions and terms of reference we formed in our childhood in response to the messages we perceived in our relationship with our parents and with our culture. Importantly, we internalised our script at a time when we did not have the experience to discern which messages to include and which ones to disregard. Without interrogating this early belief system, we repeatedly refer to it and apply it in our adult relationships, where we continue to look out at the world with very young eyes. If allowed to run its course, this early childhood script becomes the unconscious director of our life.

Disregarding our vulnerability is often part of living out of our unconscious script, which is based on idealizations about who we are supposed to be in our relationships, and who others are supposed to be. We react by pressurising ourselves to conform to a life we think we are supposed to live, where we try to mould ourselves into shapes that do not truly fit and act in ways that we think are expected of us. When we try to meet other people's expectations of us, we struggle to become our true selves. So when we feel isolated and disappointed, we pretend we are fine. We think showing strength means disregarding our vulnerability, when the opposite is the truth. Sometimes we lose faith in ourselves and settle for relationships, when deep down we know we are not honouring our true, authentic selves. We ignore the voice that tells us when a relationship is not right for us and we continue to make excuses for others. We carry on giving even when we are not listened to, appreciated, or valued. Instead of acting with compassion towards ourselves, we continue to search outside ourselves for meaning and value. Why do we do this? This is what I will explore further in this book. In particular, I am interested in connecting with the places where we can heal our hurts and find meaning and value in being our authentic selves even if this means being vulnerable. Bringing awareness, inquiry, compassion, and understanding can open this space.

With each step along this pathway to understanding relationships, I will share with you the insights and behaviours that can both transform your relationship experience and enable you to attract meaningful and responsive relationships that flourish and drop any self-limiting behavioural patterns that keep you from meeting your full relationship potential. In doing this, I will demystify the confusion that we sometimes feel when relationships go into a new territory that we do not understand. These insights are gleaned from my own inquiry into repeating patterns in my own life and from exploring fundamental psychological theories and practices about human behaviour, beliefs, and value systems.

This transformation includes:

A new awareness that supports you in placing yourself at the heart of your relationships. This means recognising and owning your own value separate from the relationship.

A movement away from reactive relationship dynamics towards proactive and responsive relationships where you are seen and you belong. This means staying connected to yourself as you relate to the other.

The development of a new relationship intelligence that supports behaviours and belief systems that are centred on self-value and self-worth.

CHAPTER 2

LIFTING THE LID ON RELATIONSHIPS

It is a joy to be hidden,
and disaster not to be found.

D.W. Winnicott

We are all unique beings. When we were born, we were whole in our innocence, vulnerability, and honesty. However, as part of our journey, we have each had to disconnect from very meaningful parts of ourselves. This is what Winnicott means as remaining hidden. By lifting the lid on our relationships, we can allow ourselves to consciously see and reconnect with our hidden parts, which we otherwise repress when they emerge in our relationships. This need for reconnection is emphasised by one of the founding fathers of psychology,

Carl Jung, who wrote that our desire to grow comes from a yearning to become whole again.

Whether we had to disconnect from the part that can speak honestly, openly, and have a sense of worth, the one that is playful and spontaneous, or the one that feels valuable and loveable, we each had to let go of parts that are unique to us. We had to push them into our unconsciousness, also known as our shadow, because they were too uncomfortable and too overwhelming for us as children to expose when our parents could not acknowledge, accept, or regard them. As a consequence, we perceived certain messages about ourselves, for example, "there is something wrong with me", "I am not OK" or "I am too much." We each have our own unique story and *life script*, as defined in the last chapter. We internalised this when our parents or other authority figures put us to the side, where we remained isolated with feelings of shame and self-doubt. We reacted by only showing the parts that were welcomed and approved. This became the script, the idealised "socially acceptable" version of our self.

Like a backpack, we carry our disconnected parts, also referred to here as our lost or hidden parts, with us. This backpack, full of unconscious life scripts, shapes our behaviours and the choices we make. Although our script is unconscious, which means it is outside our awareness, it continues to influence and direct us. Therefore, each time we suppress uncomfortable feelings or beliefs about ourselves such as, "I am not enough," they do not go away, instead, they go underground where they control us unconsciously.

We continue to bear the weight of these unconscious parts until finally we reach a place, such as heartbreak, where we become weary and we are forced to acknowledge and inquire into them. Through this inquiry we can bring these disconnected and very meaningful parts from our unconscious shadow into our awareness where we can safely meet them and be present with them once again. This process can be supported in the presence of an understanding and compassionate other, or a therapist. As part of this process, we can also loosen our rein on the protective, adapted parts that we took on in our childhood at a time when we were not regarded. These protective parts act to guard our uncomfortable feelings, but they ultimately prevent us from connecting in a compassionate and meaningful way internally with ourselves, and in our relationships with others.

It is this inquiry that heralds the beginning of our searching journey towards fulfilment and wholeness. As we search for understanding about why we get into self-compromising patterns of behaviour, we can start to bring all of these parts out from the shadow and into our awareness, for example:

The very natural and authentic part that speaks openly and honestly without fear or restriction. It hides behind the protective (censor) part that speaks from a place that seeks acceptance and regard; it fears that if it expresses itself truthfully, it will be rejected.

The vulnerable part that can express its true feelings. It hides behind the protective (strong) part that quashes feelings of hurt and disappointment when they emerge; instead it pretends that everything is fine. It fears that if it exposes its vulnerability, it will be dismissed as happened in childhood when it could not be met with compassion and understanding.

The loveable part that can experience meaning, belonging, and wholehearted connection. It hides behind words and actions. It fears that if it exposes itself, it will not be enough.

Key to building a compassionate internal relationship with ourselves is reconnecting with our vulnerable parts, which represent self-seeing, self-compassion, and self-worth. By recognising our subconscious behaviour, we can begin the process of reconnecting with our lost parts. For example, when we bring our feelings of fear, hurt, and disappointment into conscious awareness we learn the practice of tolerating our vulnerability, sense of loss, and grief without becoming overwhelmed by these feelings and dismissing them. Moreover, our very young, inner child parts experience a sense of ease as these feelings are finally given the attention and presence that they need. Consequently, we no longer need to experience these feelings as the frightening monsters that we mistakenly perceived them to be and which, up to now, we automatically tried to quash and run from.

It is through this process that we can create the foundation upon which we can build a wholehearted connection with ourselves. This inner connection can be facilitated through: compassion, a practice we learn moment by moment; by tolerating and exploring; by learning to stay with our uncomfortable feelings and becoming curious about them; by creating a conscious space that supports us in staying present with what is happening in the here-and-now; and by not automatically reacting, assuming, and taking our assumptions to be the truth. By choosing to stay with our internal experience in this way, we can inquire and ask ourselves:

Where is this feeling in my body? Can I breathe into it, and give it the breath it needs so it can open to what it wants from me? Can I tolerate holding the feeling as I breathe into it?

It is this stepping into and staying in our breath that can really hold us and support us as we open to our internal experience. Each time we practice this, we shape and strengthen a space internally where emotional presence and attunement can replace automatic and defensive behaviours.

When we cannot stay with our feelings and we get lost in what is happening, can we be compassionate towards ourselves? Can we try to see and acknowledge our very young protective parts, and the well-intentioned role they are trying to play in keeping us safe? Or do we turn on ourselves and allow our super-ego to criticise us because we got carried away in the trance of the story?

Intrinsic to building a consciousness around the relationship with ourselves is enquiring into the protective parts that we have internalised from our culture and parents, which may no longer serve us. This is referred to as our conditioning. When these parts prevent us from connecting with our vulnerability, we try to find meaning in other ways. However, as long as we allow these protective parts to run the show, we remain disconnected from our internal emotional experience. We try to find meaning in our lives by adopting external strategies, which can never bring us inner fulfilment.

Relationships can support us in reconnecting with our vulnerability. It is in the intimate relationship space we share with another that we get to shine a light on all our vulnerabilities. For this reason, we very often pick a partner because our subconscious recognises specific characteristics in him or her that can trigger our childhood wounds. We do this in the hope that these wounds will be healed and we may become whole again within and through this relationship. In this way, relationships become our greatest crucible for growth—they present us with the opportunity to recognise, acknowledge, and heal our wounded parts when they emerge. Thus, by creating a conscious and compassionate space inside, we can reconnect with, reclaim, and integrate our vulnerable and lost parts. This is integral to our journey towards wholeness where each time we do this, we become more whole, grounded, and steady. Conversely, as long as we remain disconnected from our vulnerable parts, we continue to yearn and long for these, looking to the "other" to fulfil these needs for us.

When we do not have the awareness to recognise our automatic and reactive behavioural patterns when they arise in our intimate relationships, as a relationship deepens and when these wounds show up, our tendency is to blame the other while we assume rigid positions that stem from a childhood mind-set. We think that if the relationship is right, we should not feel hurt. In this way we can get caught in a cycle of blame and recrimination rather than becoming curious and compassionate about the reality. Subsequently, we tend to go to a place where we become a much smaller version of ourselves. Whether it is putting up defensive walls, questioning everything, doubting ourselves, lowering our expectations, or losing confidence in our ability to get what we want from life. Each time we do this, we disconnect from a part of ourselves that we no longer trust. As a result, rather than growing in the relationship, we suffer, further repressing our vulnerable parts instead of reconnecting with them and integrating them.

The reality is that when something painful comes up for us, it signifies a lost part that wants to be met, understood, and integrated. I am suggesting that when we experience feelings of rejection, abandonment, hurt, disappointment, or longing, we recognise them, allow them and bear them with tenderness and understanding. This is the practice of acknowledgement and inquiry, which we can apply to each new uncomfortable feeling as it emerges. However, we can only recognise our wounded parts when we are consciously open to meeting them. When we have created a hospitable environment within ourselves where we can acknowledge all our feelings, emotions, and wounded parts, we can hold them with compassion and understanding in our own hearts. In this way, we become the nurturing parent who can soothe and comfort our wounded inner child.

Significantly, when we allow our authentic parts to emerge, we can still hold onto our protective parts that function to support us in getting things done in our day-to-day lives. We do not need to forgo these, we just need to keep an eye to them so they do not take complete charge and threaten our ability to connect emotionally and authentically in our relationships.

The Self Centred Approach

What I am calling the *Self Centred Approach* places you at the centre of your relationships, so that instead of being reactive and unconscious where you are pulled in different directions to suit others, you can remain responsive, conscious, and open to meet each new experience as it unfolds.

Deep down, each of us yearns to be taken care of by someone else. This need often overrides all else and comes into play especially in intimate relationships where we unconsciously enter the mind-set of "this person will make me whole," and "in order for this person to see me, I need to be a certain way." We adopted this mind-set as a result of the environment we grew up in where very particular terms of acceptance subconsciously applied in the early relationships that were shaped with our parents and other authority figures. When we continue to act out of a very young mind-set in our adult relationships, where we adopt particular roles in order to make ourselves more acceptable to others, our true self remains unseen and hidden. Furthermore, when we hide behind roles in our relationships, we struggle to create a true emotional connection where we can be seen, valued, and regarded. Subsequently, when we remain unseen and hidden in this area, we put our energy into blaming the other for our feelings of disappointment.

Usually there is very good reason why we hide our vulnerability, which includes our wounded child parts, in relationships. Most likely, it is because the messages that we received and/or perceived in our childhood meant that expressing our true and vulnerable selves was shameful, we learned to automatically dismiss our vulnerability just as our parents or other authority figures did, never having a good enough reason to explore why our vulnerability could not be valued. As a result, we engage in relationships in a seductive way, not giving ourselves the autonomy to act from a place of self where we have the presence to recognise our experience, the compassion to understand it and the courage to express it. Instead, we hide our vulnerability, especially from ourselves, and sadly we compromise a wholehearted connection because we cannot act from a place of worthiness, where we honour our true selves.

Thus, we continue to believe that we will only be accepted if we act out of the script we were conditioned to believe would make us acceptable as human beings. We assume that when we include our vulnerability, we will not be enough, that we will be rejected as happened when we were young. We may even drop our behaviour and play games in order to seek attention or relentlessly pursue a relationship at any cost. When somebody treats us with disregard, we step back into the relationship the minute they show up again; such is our need for acknowledgement, which takes precedence over everything else. This becomes a self-inflicted wound and an act of self-betrayal.

When we continue to engage in these behaviour and communication patterns, we can never be fulfilled because we can never allow our partner to truly see us, and vice versa. As this cycle of behaviour continues with each new relationship, we begin to lose faith in our ability to ever experience love and belonging in our relationships. We second-guess ourselves, no longer able to act with self-regard or rely on our inner trust.

At the heart of the *Self Centred Approach* is the development of a self-curious, self-compassionate, and self-seeing practice.

This helps us to build a connection with our inner selves so we can truly see and regard who we are. This is about learning how to be with the part of us that is true and unencumbered by roles, restrictions, conditions, or expectations. We can experience this part by looking inwards and connecting with our heart energy; it evokes feelings of meaning, wonder, and joy within us. It is from this inner place of connection with our hearts that our greatest source of love stems, and where we can learn to nurture, regard and consider our whole self, including our imperfect parts, which signify our humanity and our greatest window to connection with others and the world around us.

Compassion can provide the important starting point for us to ground ourselves. It enables us to connect with ourselves and others in an openhearted way where we seek to inquire, understand, meet and hold whatever is arising on our journey to wholeness, including parts that are uncomfortable such as vulnerability and neediness.

When we do not do this, we allow our subconscious fears and shadow parts to drive our reacting, avoiding, judging, blaming, or fixing behaviour. In so doing, we betray ourselves again and continue to wound our inner vulnerable child, who stays in hiding and continues to direct the show from a hidden place.

Compassion requires us to meet ourselves in an inner place of openness to what is present in our experience. By staying connected internally with our heart, our mind, and our body, we can create meaningful responses to what is happening. Becoming grounded in this way requires humility, where we can allow ourselves the space to express our true feelings of disappointment or loneliness for example, as opposed to reacting in a very automatic way where we cope without any regard for our emotional experience. When we choose to meet ourselves with compassion for who we truly are, we also allow others to see us. This is something that I will explore in more detail later.

The *Self Centred Approach* is based on self-regard, compassion, and value. It takes away the uncertainty and hurt that we often experience when we depend on others to give us these feelings. When we operate from a place of emotional presence and conscious compassionate awareness, we build inner strength; and we no longer need to depend on others for a sense of worth and value, nor do we compromise ourselves and disregard our own needs in order to fit with somebody else's expectations. Instead, we can become steady in ourselves and attract relationships that are meaningful, fulfilling, and aligned with our authentic self. Our inner vulnerable child learns that it is safe to be seen and held, and thus can relax into that holding. This means we can develop a new self-compassion, which can consciously support meaningful connections from within, as opposed to operating from an external place of hope and endless compromise. Moreover, when we nurture feelings of self-regard, we activate and allow a sense of inner purpose. Therefore, the *Self Centred Approach* supports relationships that are built on mutuality where two people can connect in a trusting and meaningful way, while at the same time remaining grounded as individuals. When this is possible, the chances are that a relationship will not just survive, but that it will flourish.

In this book I introduce you to the tools and resources that will enable you to build this conscious, compassionate, self-seeing, and self-soothing relationship with self. This allows you to tap into your internal powerhouse of emotional strength and intelligence, where you can connect with the inner wisdom and awareness that acts for your higher self. This is a transformation that will occur over time and needs to be learned and practiced. It includes developing and supporting an inner trust and regard that places self-compassion and value at the core of your actions. This supports you in developing a meaningful relationship, emotionally, psychologically and physically with yourself first and foremost, in particular:

It places you in a position where you regard yourself including your vulnerable hurts and needs, and you allow others to see and regard you.

It nurtures a connection with another where mutual support is at the forefront.

It replaces self-judgment with self-compassion.

It guides you in creating a conscious awareness and deconstructs old belief systems that no longer serve you.

It adjusts the dial on current perceptions, feelings, and behaviours that prevent you from having the relationship you want.

It supports you in developing an inner trust and self-reliance, which enables you to choose what is right for you.

CHAPTER 3

DEMYSTIFYING CONFUSING BEHAVIOURS

*Our minds work very hard to make
something out of nothing. We can perceive
silence as rejection in an instant, and then
build a cold castle on the tiny imagined brick.
The only release from the tensions we weave
around nothing is to remain a creature of the
heart. By giving voice to the river of feelings
as they flow through and through, we can
stay clear and open.*

Mark Nepo

The mind can construct a story out of nothing. However, by giving voice to the river of feelings as they flow through us, we can stay present and support ourselves in not getting lost in the story that our mind is so quick to concoct. In this chapter, I will demystify some of the feelings and behaviours that we automatically experience and engage in without conscious consideration as to what is real and what is true.

How we experience relationships has profound effects on all levels of our being: mind, body, and spirit. It is the feeling of belonging that we experience in the intimate space we create with another that surpasses most other meaningful experiences in life. Through the mirroring back we experience in this intimate space, we get a sense of the meaning we bring to the union. It is for these reasons that we experience such joy when we are in a relationship and such a feeling of loss when we can no longer be part of it. The burden of loss is more challenging and difficult when a severing occurs without any understanding as to its cause.

Coming to an understanding of the unconscious behaviours that we engage in when we enter a relationship can offer a really insightful backdrop into why we relate in the specific way we do.

As previously stated, the most important relationship we have is with ourselves. It is the inward process that we experience that has profound effects outwardly when we relate to others. Significantly, when we connect in a meaningful and compassionate way with ourselves, we develop a rich base from which we can connect in an understanding and whole-hearted way with others. In the same way, the extent to which we run from our selves, our needs, and our vulnerabilities is the extent to which we run from intimacy with others. This is a protective strategy that we developed in our childhood. It helped us to cope when we experienced painful feelings as children when we were solely dependent on our caregivers for survival. However when we continue to use this outdated strategy as adults, it impairs us when we try to form meaningful relationships.

When we enter relationships with people we are attracted to, we bring the backpack that we filled with our history with us. This is full of our unconscious needs, hopes, and expectations. In childhood we developed an attachment style and this is also part of this backpack. It hooks us at the beginning of our relationships and it also influences how we experience the other.

The architecture of our attachment style began in the relational field with our mothers and it continued to develop throughout our infancy and childhood at a time when we were wholly dependent on our parents for our survival. The interactions we experienced and the feedback we received throughout this significant relationship indicated to us whether the world is a loving and welcoming place that can be trusted, and we can relax into, or if there is something we need to be cautious about or watchful of.

Dr. Daniel Siegel states that our attachment style is developed as an outcome of the recurring experiences we had as young children with our parents[2]. This is affected by our temperament. The relationship we experience with each of our parents differs and therefore the type of attachment to one parent is independent of the other. Most profoundly, our childhood experience of these relationships greatly influences our expectations, attitudes, emotions, and actions when we enter important relationships. These first and very early relationships become the template for all other relationships.

2   Siegel, D. J. [1999]. How Relationships and the Brain Interact to Shape Who We
    Are., Guilford Publications

Neuroscience supports this early attachment theory by illustrating that our ability to connect consciously is influenced by the level of emotional attunement and nurturing we experienced in the primary relationships with our parents. This impacts on the development of the neural connections pattern in our brain and how our brain functions. Like a road map, these neural connections set out the direction we take when we enter intimate relationships and importantly, the level of vulnerability we can allow.

As explained in Chapter 2, our vulnerability is a source of strength on the journey back to reconnecting with our lost parts of self. Significantly, our ability to relate in a conscious way is indicative of our ability to connect with our vulnerability, that is, to see and allow our own vulnerability, and to also see and allow it in others. By bringing into conscious awareness the patterns of relating that we get hooked into and which prevent us from connecting with our vulnerability, we can unlock ourselves. This is what this chapter is about, understanding the roadblocks, often unconscious, that we automatically and subconsciously put in the way of connecting with our vulnerability, so that we can dismantle them.

Brené Brown defines vulnerability as *emotional risk, exposure, and uncertainty, which fuels our daily lives; it is the birthplace of innovation, creativity, and change.* Vulnerability comes from the Latin word for wound, "vulnere." It is the softest, most tender part of us. The *Self Centred Approach* invites us to come into relationship with our vulnerable parts and our wounded parts in order to hold them consciously and compassionately. It is only when we can be present with our vulnerability that we can connect in the most honest and meaningful way with ourselves primarily, and then with others. Our beauty is in our vulnerability. Our wisdom is in acknowledging and allowing it. However, our tendency is to think that there is something wrong when we feel vulnerable and experience hurt. We avoid it, mask it, or run away from it by distracting ourselves with too much busyness, for example, with work or recreationally with substances. We occupy our minds online by keeping up to date with the latest news and social media trends, and offline where we try to find meaning by continuously raising the bar so that we can be even more successful. Each time we do this, we are no longer present and open to our relational self, who is emotional, vital, and energetic.

So why do we try to shut down our vulnerable parts and most importantly why do we experience our emotions as a sign of weakness, especially when we are disappointed or hurt?

It is very possible that as vulnerable children, when we were most in need of comfort and reassurance, an uninterested or "too busy" parent instead dismissed us. If this became a pattern, then we learned that vulnerability is *bad* and needs to be dismissed and hidden. We subsequently internalised the dismissive parent who now shows up as our inner critic. So instead of allowing this tender soft part of us—our vulnerability—and being with it, we give precedence to the voice of the critic. It never wants to allow our vulnerability, it prefers to push our wounded, vulnerable parts back into the shadow where they stay hidden, and in doing so, we keep a lid on our emotions. The critic firmly holds onto the protective and defensive barriers that we constructed around our hearts. Each time we honour this critical voice and quash our vulnerable parts, which represent our source of compassion and love, we are wounded all over again, this time by ourselves. When we continue to shield ourselves and hide our tenderness and vulnerability, we search in places outside ourselves for the parts we can no longer rely on ourselves for, such as regard, value, and worth. Just like the child who continuously looks out for and relies on the gaze of its mother for love and value, we as adults, continue to look out from the child's eyes, believing that our value comes through external affirmation. We continuously look to others for feelings of love and belonging.

However, when we search outside ourselves for sources of fulfilment, our need for acknowledgement and regard supersedes everything else. We compromise the truth of who we really are, disconnecting from our authentic energy and substituting it with an idealised version of ourselves and of someone else, for whom we develop unhealthy attachments and expectations. The critic, who does not have compassion but does have control, moulds this idealised part. Subsequently, we also hope that the idealised other in the relationship will take care of us. When we project our needs and wants onto somebody else and we expect them to be met, we are setting ourselves up for disappointment and heartbreak. Moreover, when the connections we form are based on ideas of who we take ourselves to be and who we want the other person to be, we fail to form any true emotional connection in our relationships. Instead we relate in an *object-to-object* way to the other person, as opposed to a *true-self-to-true-self* way.

When we constantly look to others for reassurance and a sense of value, we confirm that we do not and cannot rely on ourselves. Each time we do this, we fire up our stress response.

As children, we did not have the developed emotional resources to self-soothe. We depended on our parents to provide the emotional support that we needed to help us to manage our emotions. If our parents were consistently able to provide this comfort and affirmed that our feelings were welcome, we developed the neural architecture of self-soothing and self-regulation in that first relational imprint. Conversely, if they consistently shamed or dismissed us for being emotional, tearful, or sad, we learned that these feelings were *bad*, so we feared and avoided them, and we adapted behaviours that were perceived as *good*. However, when we did not get the nurturing we needed to build internal emotional supports and neural pathways for ourselves, as adults, when we experience painful or difficult feelings, fear continues to activate our nervous system, causing us to panic. This brings about feelings of "I cannot cope," "I am not good enough," or "I am unlovable" and consequently, old wounds are reopened.

Neuroscience explains that if we are not comfortable with feeling hurt, we flee from our vulnerability and our compassionate source and we ignite the stronger, primitive old brain, known as the *amygdala*, which focuses on danger and survival. When it experiences mistrust which, for example, someone looking a certain way at us may trigger, it acts to control, defend, and attack. In doing so, it activates the *flight, fight,* or *freeze* stress response. In *Buddha's Brain*, Rick Hanson and Richard Mendius explain that when we activate our acute stress response, we make it extremely difficult, if not impossible, to remain receptive to other parts of our brain. As long as the survival brain, the *amygdala*, is in control, our nervous system is activated and our rational new brain, the *neocortex*, which regulates our emotions, is short-circuited. In short, if we live in a fear-based, defensive, and controlled way, we are reacting with the primitive brain, as opposed to responding from the rational new brain.

This new brain, the *neocortex* can help us to put things into perspective and context, while the old survival brain gives authority to our inner critic, who exaggerates or catastrophises situations, creating stories that keep us fearful. It puts us in the mind, where in the words of Mark Nepo, *we create something out of nothing*. Our *amygdala* immediately triggers fear signals when it suspects a threat of rejection or loss. The more we activate this old survival response, the more we experience feelings of isolation, and the less we experience feelings of intrinsic connectedness or belonging.

Underpinning our strategy to avoid pain is Richard Schwarz's *Internal Family Systems* model. This model sets out that we each developed protector parts, which are well intentioned and come to our rescue when we experience uncomfortable feelings. For example, they support us when we need to create distance in an unhealthy relationship. However, when it comes to intimacy, these subconscious parts become ill-advised adversaries whose only objective is to keep the status quo and to create barriers to anything that makes us feel uncomfortable. Ultimately they restrict us from growing in our relationships.

Our protector parts stem from our subconscious. We adapted them at a time when we needed their protection. However, until they can be brought into conscious awareness, they assume we still need their protection. They appear when we enter the intimate relationship sphere, which is a place that asks of us to open to the other by connecting with our vulnerability. However, when a younger protector part associates vulnerability with a past hurt, it steps in. As a consequence, instead of experiencing the relationship with presence, and from a place of here-and-now reality, we subconsciously become identified with the part that seeks to protect us. That is, we give authority to the part, without questioning its position, stance, or belief system. In effect, we unwittingly and unconsciously allow our adult self to take a back seat while this younger part takes charge of the *reality* we now find ourselves in.

Our protector part is the inner critic who tries to keep us safe. However, it often shows up under the guise of a judge, a blamer, or one who adopts a false sense of independence by running away or hiding behind protective masks. Although this vigilant practice stems from a very real place of wounding, the defence mechanism is dysfunctional because it subconsciously applies past childhood experiences and behaviours to present circumstances. It assumes that we cannot cope, and so the continuous relationship patterns of frustration and disappointment continue. Whether our inner critic associates intimate relationships with a place of emotional inflexibility where we will be stifled, or it wants to protect us from abandonment, rejection, or shame, it unwittingly intrudes on our relationships uninvited. Like an overprotective parent who struggles to allow their child the freedom to grow, our inner critic feels the need to continually protect us. In *Self-Therapy*, the psychologist Jay Earley maintains that these protector parts often have neither finesse nor flexibility and they only know how to do one thing, regardless of the situation. This creates difficulties in our relationships because when we allow this intrusion, we become identified with the critic. We run, internally by shutting down our vulnerability, and externally by creating emotional and physical distance in our relationships.

While our protector parts have positive intent, we need to discern and question their protective strategies in our reality as adults. We can only acknowledge their intent, and the strategies they are using to protect us, when we are open to recognising them, and then holding them with a sense of curiosity. By bringing intentionality and presence to our experience we enable ourselves to catch these parts when they show up and then bring them into consciousness. Through this practice, we open to observing our rising emotions and our protectors as they move into play. Thus, we become a third party observer to our own behaviour. Sometimes it is the voice that says, "I am not good enough." It happens when our subconscious associates a particular behaviour with an old childhood wound. In other cases, we sometimes compound the inner critic who says, "I am not good enough" by continuing to engage in relationships where the other self-identifies with their parts, and as a result they cannot regard us properly. In this situation, we have two people viewing, interpreting, and reacting to the world through a younger, outmoded lens that may not reflect the reality of the situation.

By allowing our vulnerability to emerge we can access our compassion where we can hold these wounds with kindness and understanding. So when an uncomfortable feeling or the voice of "I am not good enough" emerges, we can compassionately acknowledge and allow it. We can soothe the part that hurts by placing a hand on the heart, breathing in through the heart and saying,

I know it is hard, I am here for you,
I believe in you. You are more than enough.

When our discomfort is too much, we can nurture it by taking ourselves away and entering an environment that we associate with inner healing and nourishment. This can simply mean going for a walk, connecting with nature or listening to soothing music. By learning to hold our painful feelings in this way, we awaken the new brain, especially the *hippocampus*. This part of the *limbic* brain can support us in discerning and modifying older representations of our self and others. Importantly, we no longer identify with the inner vulnerable child that cannot cope as we can now soothe and emotionally support ourselves.

Like anything that we give our focused attention to, we can now begin to experience a sense of ease when we relate to our uncomfortable feelings. Like the child who needs to be held and reassured with love and compassion, our uncomfortable feelings or lost parts emerge because they want to be held, understood, integrated, and belong. It is only when our uncomfortable feelings can be met with openness and understanding that a sense of ease can emerge. In the opposite way, when we try to quash these feelings or move to a place of *narrative* about them, we believe the *narrative* and take it to be the truth. Moreover, when we do not interrogate our uncomfortable feelings, they become more anxious and our protective mechanisms, in particular, the voice of our inner critic becomes louder and more difficult to ignore.

As we learn to remain connected internally with our emotions, we allow and hold ourselves in our vulnerability. By opening up a space within our self, we can ask,

Is this really true? Have I reached rock bottom
and I cannot cope on my own?

This process recognises the inner child who seeks support and cultivates the part of us that can grow an internal parent who has compassion. By creating an internal dialogue and inner inquiry, we give voice to our own internal nurturing parent who regards and understands the inner child and regards her vulnerability by speaking to the inner critic, who acts to protect, by saying for example,

I know how hard you have worked to protect me. You
helped me to survive at a time when I needed you and
I could not expose my vulnerability. I really appreciate
your help. It is safe for me to connect with my own

vulnerability now, and it is time for me to
honour who I really am.

By acknowledging our inner critic for the role it has worked hard to accomplish, and by giving it permission to step back, we can allow our vulnerable part to step forward. It can now be recognised and appreciated for the valid place it has as part of our being. When we nurture this practice, we learn to rely more on ourselves and we naturally learn to manage our emotions. Thus, we no longer inflict wounds on ourselves or give voice to the one who says "I am not good enough" each time we experience difficult feelings such as shame, rejection, resentment, hurt, or betrayal. When we act with compassion, we nurture our own sense of secure attachment. This is the real act of self-love and the cornerstone of the *Self Centred Approach.*

Summary

The early relational dynamics that we developed in our child-hood form the building blocks for how we will engage in our adult relationships. When we got the nurturing that we needed as children, we developed a secure attachment style where we could remain conscious and emotionally attuned in our relationships. However, when we did not or could not experience the nurturing and holding that we needed, we learned to distrust our own integrity and this doubt continues in a consistent way in our adult relationships. Therefore, when we experience uncomfortable feelings, our tendency is to turn away from ourselves and become identified with our inner critic and with the strategies we used in the past that protected us. While we continue to become identified with its voice, we live in a distorted reality where growth is restricted.

When we learn to nurture and welcome our vulnerable feelings and when we no longer need to flee from our lost or wounded parts, we can begin to hold and nurture ourselves with compassion and understanding. It is through this practice that we develop new neural pathways to self-love and compassion. This practice allows the protective parts to relax and to become more at ease. They will still show up but when we are open to recognising them, we can hold them with a new understanding. In this way we can awaken to our inner self and no longer become identified with the protective parts.

By allowing and holding a compassionate presence in the relationship with our selves first and then with the other, we provide the key to opening to our vulnerability. This is our true source of love.

CHAPTER 4

ROMANTIC ATTRACTION

*In the longing and possession of romantic love, it is
as if the body has been loaned to someone else but
has then from some remote place, taken over the
senses—we no longer know ourselves. Longing calls for
a beautiful, grounded humiliation; the abasement of
what we thought we were and strangely, the giving
up of central control while being granted a watchful,
scintillating, peripheral discrimination.*

David Whyte

David Whyte speaks for the need for a "grounded humiliation" that occurs in the sacred longings between two people.
Attraction draws us towards another suddenly, inexplicably,

and humbly. Romantic love asks us to connect with our vulnerability, a necessary humiliation that enables us to truly emerge through the expression of the true and raw holding energy of the heart. The profound quality of being recognised by a significant other awakens feelings of longing deep within us, and more than anything we want to stay in the relationship. Suddenly we feel whole, energised, "at home". However, when we unwittingly and unconsciously associate romantic love with idealised portrayals of who we take ourselves to be, and who we take the other person to be, we adopt a relational style that comes from a subconscious and automatic place where we may not always act in our best interests. Importantly when we continue with automatic behaviours, beliefs, and expectations, they stay in our subconscious shadow where they remain unexplored. In this way, we cannot take responsibility for our actions because we are acting outside our awareness, where we can never truly allow ourselves the opportunity to experience heartfelt fulfilment. This chapter is about lifting the lid on the subconscious beliefs and values that we attribute to romantic relationships and bringing them into consciousness.

When our interpretation of romantic love speaks to the idealised version of our self that we think we *should* be, we unconsciously remain hidden. A very young part of us mistakenly thinks that if we take down our guard and show our softest most tender parts, there will be nothing there to hold us together. However, as emphasised in the last chapter, when we hide our vulnerability, there is no possibility for an emotional connection to develop. Without a true and honest connection, a relationship cannot grow; this is quintessentially what the *Self Centred Approach* upholds. As long as we continue to identify with the romantic story that we project onto the relationship, where only our idealised parts can be allowed and displayed, we continue the mythology of an *object-to-object*, as opposed to *true-self-to-true-self* meeting. As a result, we create distance from the true essence of who we are, as our self is left out of the picture. We also do not present the other person with our true unedited self.

Choosing to meet our true wholehearted selves is an act of courage and self-compassion where we can forgive ourselves for being imperfect. We do this when we can hold, acknowledge, and nurture with compassion our vulnerabilities, no longer trying to quash, hide, and run from them. It is only by opening and seeking to understand our feelings in this conscious and compassionate way, that we can truly open to our partner.

Conversely, when we are too scared to connect with our vulnerability, we present ourselves in a very particular way in the relationship by only showing our idealised or masked selves. Our mind believes this to be an effective strategy because we do not risk exposing our imperfections, where our humility stems from.

In order to understand our interpretation of romance and the behaviours we automatically adopt in this relational space, it is important to revisit the lens through which our ideas about romantic love were first formed. These ideas have been moulded in a very specific way, which began in our childhood when we were captivated by fairy tales where the prince or the hero would show up as the one true saviour. He would give his princess everything, love, riches, and a castle. Ultimately they would live happily ever after—The End! Although the fairy tale only reflects the beginning of the love story, this idyllic perception of romance continues to captivate us on a subconscious level, and re-establishes itself each time we are exposed to romantic depictions of love. In today's society, idealised portrayals of romantic love are taken to an extreme level where seductive marketing suggests a very prescribed and contrived narrative about the requirements for romantic love, what it represents, and how to attract it.

As a consequence, we subsequently form ideas about where to place value and emphasis in this emotional, spiritual, psychological, and physical context, where our tendency is to operate in relational dynamics where we are not really present or indeed conscious. Our wish to be desired by our partner, or to see him or her in a particular way, takes precedence.

By staying attached to the idealistic lens through which we view romance, we construct relationships where only masked or false qualities or projections are portrayed. For example:

We subconsciously project the mother or father image on to our partner, where we replay our childhood experience in the hope that this time we will be seen and acknowledged.

We create a fantasy about the person we are with. We do not engage in the relationship space in a present or conscious way where we can allow ourselves to experience what we are seeing, hearing, and feeling. Instead we project a sentimental image onto ourselves and onto our partner.

By operating within these dynamics, we are not truly present in the relationship. Instead, we are relating in an *object-to-object* way, where we are relating to the projections that we have superimposed onto the other, unconsciously taking the projections to represent the real him or her. In turn the other in the relationship is also relating to projections placed on us, that is, who he or she takes us to be. When we bring our unconscious behaviours into awareness we allow ourselves to discern between what is real and what is fantasy. To begin this process, it is important to understand why the feelings of belonging that we experience when we enter relationships manifest in such a profound way.

Psychologists believe that during the first few months of our lives we shared a profound spiritual and physical connection with our mother. This was a symbiotic relationship so profound that we did not realise we were a distinct being, separate from our mother; we experienced a merged state with no awareness of internal divisions between our thoughts, feelings, and actions, and those of our mother. We were merged with mother and this merged state represents our first template of connection, it is the place where our longing stems from.

As we developed a sense of independence, part of us still yearned to be connected with our mother in the deeply unifying and spiritual way we had once experienced. When we enter a romantic relationship, these same merged feelings and longings arise. The yearning for those early emotional bonds and feelings of wholeness is reignited, as once again we sense a unique and meaningful connection with another person. This explains why the "in love" phase is euphoric; a very deep unseen part of us recognises specific qualities in a very distinct other, which we subconsciously associate with our primary attachment figure. The experience of identifying very meaningful parts in others can be so profound that the attraction can overtake us. We sense that a relationship with this person can provide the healing crucible where we can be truly seen, and the relationship will support us in becoming whole again. In our partner, we imagine we have found our pathway *home*.

Harville Hendrix, a psychologist who has spent a lifetime researching relationship dynamics, supports this philosophy.

We are born in relationship, we are wounded in relationship, and we can be healed in relationship.

He developed an *Imago Theory*[3], which posits that we are drawn to characteristics in others that resemble our primary care givers. It is the familiarity of these characteristics that allows us to be relaxed enough to feel the attraction. The intensity of the attraction depends on the number of similar traits that our partner has to our primary care giver. Existentially, it is the negative effect of these traits that creates the dominant force in the attraction. These traits represent the lost parts of ourselves that we try to reclaim when we enter a new relationship. They only come to the fore at a later point in the relationship. Our drive for attachment is driven by our desire to become whole again. We sense that our partner has also recognised something very unique in us too. The feeling of being seen in this intimate way resonates in a very primal place within us. When this happens, we connect with a lost or forgotten part of ourselves, a part that may not have been met adequately as a child.

The Imago Theory explains how our very first and most profound relationship with our early attachment figure (mother) shapes our attachment style. We are hooked

3   Hendrix, H. [2008]. Getting the Love You Want., St. Martin's Press

initially when we recognise very specific characteristics in another that resemble the attachment style of this primary relationship. At a subconscious level, we unwittingly confuse our lover with our parent and we interpret some promise of being held in a healing way by our partner, taking him or her to be our saviour, the one who really sees us and who can make us whole. In doing so, we inadvertently pile pressure on the relationship, even at its fledgling stage. Moreover, our subconscious need and desire to be in a relationship is so strong that it drives the relationship and we continue to stay, even when we are not seen, held, or healed.

To better understand our distinct drivers for attraction, let us revisit the child's eye view of the world, which is simplistic and grandiose. The child believes that everything is his or her fault, so "*if mother does not love me, it is my fault. I am bad. If I do it enough, in this way, she will love me.*" Significantly, when the child is dismissed or disapproved of, the inner voice of "there is something wrong with me" or "I am not good enough" quickly emerges. When we enter relationships, our subconscious mind thinks that if we can replay a very particular episode of our childhood, we can change the outcome, and in so doing, we can heal our wounded parts and become whole again. However, when the opposite happens, and we allow our inner critic to take charge, old childhood wounds are reopened. Thus, by continuing to hand over authority to the critic in this way, we cannot consciously acknowledge, hold, and soothe our feelings as adults. Instead, the hurt we experience is deep. Consequently, the relationship becomes a place of anguish. This is the unconscious bind that we, as adults, find ourselves in when we continue to look at the world through the subconscious eyes of the child.

This helps us to understand why the child of an emotionally avoidant parent is attracted to an emotionally avoidant partner, or sometimes we may be drawn to partners with dependency issues such as alcohol for the same reasons. We believe that now that we are in adult we can shape the relationship so that this time round we can be acknowledged properly and loved. This relationship can hold us and we can change or rewrite the script. However, the subconscious yearning to become whole again in this way often trips us up as we re-enact the scene over and over again with each new partner in the hope that the outcome will eventually change. As long as we adopt this subconscious behaviour, we continue to recycle the same unsuccessful relational dynamics.

So what is it about each of us that determines very specific experiences and patterns of behaviour when we enter relationships? To unpack this question, let us take a look at the circumstances in which we selected the bricks we used to construct our identity, and the bricks that we rejected. Our constructed identity represents the terms of acceptance, which we developed in our childhood in response to the messages we received in the relationship with our parents. It houses the definitions we subsequently formed about the world and how we could be accepted and valued in it. Therefore, our sense of value and worth very often remains associated with the identity we developed at a time when we did not have the freedom to be ourselves.

As a consequence, very meaningful parts of ourselves had to be pushed into the shadow because when we exposed them, they were rejected or dismissed, they were too much for our guardians to tolerate. We subconsciously continue to keep these parts in the shadow when we enter intimate relationships, where we automatically associate intimacy with showing up in a superficial way, only revealing our constructed or masked parts. We do this when we present ourselves to others in an idealised way. Sometimes, in order to illustrate this, we associate ourselves with particular images, people, or objects that we perceive as desirable but which deep down, do not represent the true version of who we really are. For example, we may have constructed the image of *independent* woman or man in order to mask a very young needy part. The *independent* mask may be what initially attracted our partner, however, when our needy self emerges, a different dynamic is experienced in the relationship. Our partner, who was attracted to our *independent* woman or man projection, may experience disappointment or a sense of loss, and may react by running for cover or disappearing.

This is what happens in various ways when we invite our partner to connect with a constructed or untrue version of ourselves. We do not allow our true self to be exposed, only the conditioned parts, which we learned to adopt in order to be acceptable. Each time we invite our partner to connect with us in this way, we consequently deny him or her from really seeing us. As a result, there is always a part of us that is working against us having the love or relationship we most desire.

When we operate from the conditioned self, we also inadvertently deny ourselves from seeing our partner, whom we view through a very conditioned lens where only very specific parts can be seen. Thus, if we were conditioned to only esteem certain idealistic or tangible qualities in a partner, when we enter relationships with somebody in whom we associate these qualities, we create an idealistic and often exaggerated story about him or her. Consequently we fail to truly see our partner because when we regard our partner as an *object* onto which we project idealised qualities and emotions, the relationship is built from a foundation of *object-to-object* projections, instead of *true-self-to-true-self.* For example, we may be attracted to somebody because we admire his or her work ethic. Initially we are drawn to their very dynamic approach, professionalism, and commitment to work, we see these attributes as honourable. However, as the relationship progresses, we may come to realize that our partner's work takes precedence over us and we slowly begin to resent the quality that first attracted us to him or her. When we develop attachments to the idealised qualities we project on to the other, we often get drawn into relationships where:

We undermine our own needs in an effort to stay in the relationship.

We get lost in a place of attachment, placing emphasis on particular idealised qualities. In turn, we lose our sense of self for the sake of being with the other, even if we are unhappy.

This explains why we are often attracted to partners who have opposite traits to us; for example the quiet and reserved person is drawn to someone who is outgoing and jovial. In our search for wholeness, we recognise traits in others that we perceive will complete us. However, when we inadvertently regard these others in whom we recognise our lost parts as our source of happiness, our minds can create stories and assumptions that are often overstated. Sometimes we cling to these perceived *good* or benign qualities and attributes and do not want to let them go. We create an expectation that if we are with this person:

We will be worthwhile and have value.

He or she can protect us, see us, and make us whole.

By awakening to consciousness and by understanding that when we identify qualities in another that we cling to, deep down we recognise in our partner a lost part of us, which draws us to him or her. Whether our lost part represents one who is playful, emotional, or contemplative, we sense that the other has something that can make us whole again. However, what we are attracted to in our partner represents a very meaningful lost part that we have projected onto him or her. When we recognise this, we can acknowledge the part and integrate it. Thus, when we turn our focus inwards, we can shift from a place of searching externally to place of inner connection and presence where we take another step closer to wholeness.

Recognising parts in others that arouse feelings of longing in us is an essential part of the searching journey we go on in order to be complete again. This is why intimate relationships provide such an effective way for us to identify and connect with our lost parts. Thus, relationships become a crucible for growth where we acknowledge and integrate our lost parts; and a crucible for differentiation where we differentiate from the constructed and idealised self we show the world, and allow a very true and meaningful version to unfold and be seen.

As part of this unfolding, we remove the idealised masks that we subconsciously projected onto our partner and begin to connect in a much truer way with their humanity.

Conversely, when we cling to our ideas and projections about a relationship, as opposed to experiencing the other in the relationship from a real and grounded place, we allow something or somebody else to take control over us. When relationships are built on projections and false imaginings, we step out of ourselves and we act from a place of disconnection, where we no longer regard our true selves. Instead we relinquish our own sense of purpose and value, for the sake of the idealised other, and in doing so we distance ourselves from experiencing true happiness. Hence, when we associate desirability with how successful someone is, we get blinkered by successful attributes and we become attached to what they represent, and we also get side-tracked from getting our own needs met.

When we consider somebody to be hugely desirable, there is a subconscious tendency to consider him or her better than us. We are seduced by the idea that this person will elevate me or make me better than I am. In such relationships we can experience a level of self-esteem and validation based on the romantic and sentimental projections we place on the other. However, we can lose sight of our own self-value, inner fulfilment and purpose; and get lost in a false sense of fantasy.

Before we know it, the relationship dynamic quickly changes to a position of imbalance where our boundaries become enmeshed in the attachment we have created. We adopt the very vulnerable position of "I am not OK, but you are OK" where we unwittingly align our energy with being accepted and regarded by our partner.

When this behaviour manifests itself, there is no room for the part of us that is acting in this way to identify this as a pattern. We lose sight of our own needs and forget to ask ourselves important questions such as, "Am I being valued?", "Is this relationship good for me as a person?", and "If not, why not?" Consequently, when there can be no curiosity about the other in the relationship, a true and intimate connection cannot be sustained, or indeed formed.

The inescapable consequence of such vulnerable relationship dynamics is disappointment. It quickly enters the fray when something we have longed for is taken from us or an expectation is not met. Our subconscious tries to protect us by avoiding our painful feelings and distancing us from our vulnerability. But when we try to avoid our pain, we cannot hold or be compassionate towards ourselves. Instead, we project *bad* person and blame onto our partner for not meeting our needs, saving us, or making us whole. Rather than meeting our disappointment, holding it, and allowing it, we blame and judge the other and love suddenly becomes hate, as the person we idealised is now the *bad* person.

The truth is that we inevitably undertake the consequences of disappointment each time we enter a romantic relationship. In order to enter the uncharted and mysterious terrain of wholeness, we are being asked to relinquish control of our own hearts. This requires a letting go of our identity and a humbling of the self we thought was invulnerable. So when a relationship lights up all of our vulnerabilities and lost parts, which include feelings of unworthiness and not being seen, we can turn compassionately towards these parts, hold them, and own them for ourselves. This is a process that requires courage so we can allow our feelings of disappointment and trust ourselves enough to stand in our own humility, and humanity. It is from this compassionate place where we connect with our hearts that we can truly grow. Making conscious our true feelings by experiencing our vulnerability is a very necessary part of opening to an awakened heart and an awakened life. Conversely, each time we turn away from our vulnerability, we turn away from ourselves and from the one we love. When we armour ourselves in blame, judgment, or resentment, we lose the opportunity to connect with the true essence of who we really are, and who our partner is. We opt instead to replace our disappointment with a false sense of authority and independence, where instead of exploring our feelings, we instead construct a story about the other.

In an ideal world, we would all act from a place of inner connection and presence where our relationships would develop in a conscious and meaningful way. However, very often our internal systems for experiencing feelings of self-esteem and value are based on exaggerated romantic qualities that we project onto our partner. When we become attached to these projections, we lose sight of the true version.

When the approach we take comes from a place of inner feeling and attunement, where emotionally and psychologically we can remain grounded and whole, we can experience our relationships in a very present and honest way. By turning our energy inwards and focusing on our true feeling experience and heart energy, we shift from a place of searching externally to an internal place of connection with the self where we can meet our lost parts, no longer clinging to or depending on others for these parts. In this way, relationships can provide the healing experience to heal our wounds, where, as each new part is identified, owned, named, and articulated, it can be held, nurtured, and reintegrated once again. Importantly, by holding ourselves in this conscious and compassionate way, we put ourselves in a position where we can discern whether or not a true connection with our partner is viable. This is the essence of the *Self Centred Approach*.

Summary

As very young children, we each adapted roles and constructed identities in the intimate relationships within our families. In these early relational experiences, we selected the bricks that were worthy and the ones that needed to be shunned. This process formed our relationship structure. It follows that when we enter intimate relationships, we subconsciously identify with the identities we constructed in our childhood where we abided by our parents' terms of acceptance. We continue to believe, as adults, that these early identities represent our value and worth.

We alone determine our behaviour within relationships, and the power of our behaviours and actions has profound consequences. As long as we continue to operate from a sub-conscious place, we can never acknowledge the automatic patterns, the default positions we adopt and the beliefs that no longer serve us.

When a true emotional connection is absent within a relationship, we often compromise and go to a place of story-telling, telling ourselves that a relationship with this idealised partner will provide the feelings of value and love that we long for. However, in this subconscious reality, we base our perception of the relationship on sentimental and idealistic projections as opposed to experiencing the relationship with emotional presence. Subsequently, we take on an *object-to-object* dynamic as opposed to a *true-self-to-true-self* seeing and connecting.

As the *Self Centred Approach* upholds, we can only develop a true and meaningful connection with another when we have built a true and meaningful connection with ourselves where we are present and connected with our vulnerability and authentic self. This includes our self-sabotaging self, our blaming self, and our hidden needy self.

CHAPTER 5

POSITIVE REGARD

*Your task is not to seek for love, but merely to
seek and find all the barriers within yourself that
you have built against it.*

Rumi

Love asks us to regard the true expression of our hearts. As
Rumi suggests, this is a quest that requires us to lift the barriers and walk through the opening to our authenticity, an
act that requires courage where we choose to acknowledge
and surrender to our feelings, no longer running from or
hiding them.

As discussed in the last chapter, when we enter romantic
relationships a very meaningful and intuitive part of us experiences wonder and awe as a doorway to self-discovery and

fulfilment has suddenly been opened. We sense that a relationship with this particular other will enable us to become whole again. Consequently, our need to be regarded in the relationship becomes very important. However, when we live in a small story about who we are and who we need to be in order to be seen, to belong, and to be regarded, we act in ways that compromise our true essence. By keeping our humility and true nature hidden we inadvertently stand in our own way of connecting in a meaningful way, and vice versa.

In order to understand why our need for regard is so important, and how we can attain it without falling victim to it, let's take a look at how relationships play such a fundamental role in our participation in and experience of life.

We are social beings and like trees, birds and bees, we too are grounded in nature. Bees communicate with each other to form highly efficient hives, birds flock together to form protective communities where every member is accounted for; and trees are capable of friendships that go so far as to feed and nurture each other. In his book, *The Hidden Life of Trees*, Peter Wohlleben writes about the affection trees share with each other. The strength of their connection equates to the level of support they provide to each other. It is the same for us. We are mammals with a high social need. We too come together with others and form supportive relationships in order to survive.

Our humanity draws us to each other. Just as a baby's vulnerability instils in us a desire to protect, suffering evokes in us a need to support. Our instinct is to connect with others. As previously mentioned, our basic psychological need is to be regarded and to belong; this forms one of the basic tenets of Maslow's hierarchy of needs. A ballast to this theory is the fact that in earlier societies, not belonging meant not surviving. To be cast out by the tribe meant certain death. This fear of isolation and alienation is deeply written in the DNA and structure of our nervous systems. Thus, there is a constant need to belong and to be safe in our belonging.

Fear of not belonging still triggers our old brain's survival mode, which is always linked to keeping the status quo and keeping us safe. This primitive part of our brain is based on fear and the negative bias. When we experience the feeling of being outside a group, we are held hostage by the need to belong. However, sometimes the price we pay to belong is too high and we suffer the sharp consequences of disconnection from our real needs, values, and longings. We forget that the first belonging must be to ourselves, and then the group; this lies at the core of the *Self Centred Approach*. It is about making ourselves whole first, where we can rely on a sense of inner trust and presence for ourselves just as we are, and not the self that was constructed to belong to our families, to culture, and the community. As long as we feel that we need to belong to the tribe our sense of value comes from the need to be externally accepted and to belong. We therefore become dependent on others for feelings of wholeness and worth. The questions I am asking here are:

Can we become *Self Centred*, so that we place our self at the centre?

Are we looking to belong to something that is not aligned to our true self?

Can we become conscious of what we are bringing into the relationship in terms of attachment style, needs and expectations?

Is the price we pay to belong to this relationship too high? Do we have to give up too much of ourselves?

Are we expecting another to make us whole? What are the unconscious projections that we are putting on our partner? Can we do the work of making these conscious?

To answer these questions it is important to revisit our childhood, the place where we first learned about regard.

As babies and children, we were wholly dependent on our parents to take care of us. Not only did we depend on them to feed and bathe us, but also how they held and cuddled us, played with us, read to us, and nurtured us, evoked feelings of belonging. When our parents could support us emotionally we felt a sense of value. In order to continue experiencing these feelings as we developed, our need for positive regard became hugely important; our sense of value and inner worth was dependent upon it.

As a result, the level of regard we experienced in our childhood and how hard we had to work for it comes into play when we form relationships. In other words, how we were regarded in our family forms the blueprint for how we perceive ourselves in relationships and how we perceive others in them. Although our strategies for getting regard were formed at a time when we were impressionable children, we continue to automatically apply very young perceptions, expectations, and understandings about regard in our adult lives. To make conscious and awaken to our out-dated childhood pro-gramme, it is important to look back with adult eyes at our much younger selves.

As children we saw our parents as big giants in our world. We relied on them as our authority and we depended solely on them for a sense of how we were met in the world. When they told us something, we were programmed to believe it; we did not have the resources to question or challenge their programming. As a result, the conditioning we received from them shaped our view of the world and our view of who we are in the world. Therefore, how we were seen in our family is hugely indicative of how we see ourselves and the qual-ity of the experiences we have with others, just as the family systems that our parents grew up in greatly influenced their view of the world and hence, their parenting style.

Implicit rules and behaviours are often passed down from generation to generation. When these views are distorted and parents can only see their children through their own lens of low self-worth, they project feelings of "not good enough" or "not worthy of" onto them. As a result, the emotional support that is required to nurture their children's feelings of inherent value is instead substituted by idealistic expectations where only certain behaviours and performance standards are acceptable, without any consideration given to nurturing self-worth through emotional presence and support. For example, sometimes being part of a family value system means it is not possible to confidently have a voice, express an opinion, or ask questions; children are "seen and not heard". In other cases, emotions are met with dismissal or rejection. Carl Rogers, the founding figure of *client-centred therapy*, believed that when such value systems exist in families, they take away from a child's freedom and natural propensity to experience the world.

As children, when we were not given the emotional support we needed to develop our own emotional value base, we developed coping strategies. These were our early survival mechanisms and they would enable us to find a way of being regarded. We sought this regard by behaving in ways that were acceptable and of value to our parents. This sometimes meant that we could not express how we truly felt because we realised that it was more important to adhere to our family value system and expectations. As a consequence, we covered up our intrinsic selves. We constructed masks that showed the *good* parts and we hid the parts that could not be allowed, pushing them into our shadow. This was essentially the cost of *belonging*.

Very often, our gender dictated the messages we received. For example, a woman assumed a caring role, and a man could not show any sign of weakness or vulnerability. Some of us thought that our value came from looking after other people's needs and disregarding our own. In other cases, it was not possible to make choices and instead decisions were imposed upon us. Sometimes the behavioural dynamics in our family were so defensive that no matter how hard we worked to seek regard, the messages we received were confusing and sometimes bewildering. When this was our experience, we struggled to feel any sense of inner worth and value; we felt knocked back, unsteady, and unsure of how we were met in the world. Consequently we developed a very limited sense of our true and inherent value.

In order to try and fit into and belong to our family system, we reacted to our environment by adopting certain performance standards, behaviours and belief systems. For example, if our parents were not supportive or encouraging, and were instead critical or controlling, the likelihood was that we could not allow ourselves the freedom to trust our feelings or act with any sense of inner authority; we were taught that it had to be sought. As a result, we then became self-critical and from a very young place the voice of "there is something wrong with me" and "I am not (good) enough," began to grow. This voice was confirmed each time we were rejected. The experience of not being acknowledged or regarded when we exposed our true nature was so painful that we disconnected from it. It was easier to quash our feelings and no longer expose that part of us. We constructed a protective shell, which we could hide behind and meet the world with, dissociating ourselves from our true authentic and spontaneous nature, our vulnerability.

As I already alluded to, our vulnerability is our connection to our full humanity. When we allow our vulnerability to be revealed, we allow the essential emotional connection that we each need in order to wholeheartedly participate in life. This connection allows us to experience feelings such as courage, self-compassion, trust, value, and love. Therefore, a huge consequence of isolating ourselves from our vulnerability is that our internal feelings of value and belonging cannot be nurtured or enriched; we have to find another supply.

We do this by leveraging our sense of value on how we are acknowledged by others. We self-question when we are not treated with the regard we hoped for and we compromise ourselves in order to try to gain regard and feel valued. Even though we may present a mask of strength and independence to the world, at heart we believe that we are flawed.

Deep inside us is a very young child who was shamed for being needy, for being fearful and for being vulnerable. When this child learned it was not possible to trust the emotional space where they tried to find understanding, reassurance, and love, they protected themselves from further annihilation by repressing their vulnerable feelings. Sadly without any emotional resources, the child believed the shameful message they perceived about themselves when they exposed their vulnerability, and internalised the shaming and dismissing as theirs.

Hiding our vulnerability was necessary at a time when we needed protection. However, as adults we mistakenly and unconsciously continue with these childhood beliefs about ourselves, thinking that we will only be acceptable if we are seen in a particular way, for example, "as a good person," "a hard-working person" or a "successful person."

Truly loving, belonging, and feeling worthy of love, necessitates us to be courageous and once again inhabit and own our vulnerability. Conversely, as long as we keep our vulnerability in the shadow, we stay disconnected from our emotional source. We do this each time we shield ourselves from a conscious place of feeling and experiencing. For example, we deny ourselves the true expression of our hurt, believing this circumvention to be a form of strength. However, each time we run from our feelings when they emerge, we commit the ultimate deception to ourselves. When we remain separate from our most precious and meaningful parts in this way, we believe that we cannot cope on our own. Moreover, we continue to keep our feelings in the shadow where they continue to control our unconscious patterns of longing, expectation, and life decisions. Consequently, we remain in the unconscious script that we need another to complete us, and we continue to live a smaller, shrunken version of our life.

This particularly comes into play when we enter an intimate relationship and the connection we form with our partner awakens our vulnerability, which has not been able to experience feelings of self-worth and value from its own source. Our inner vulnerable child becomes exhilarated by the very unique feelings of connection and belonging it experiences in this intimate experience, and subconsciously, we identify our partner as the *saviour* who can truly hold and heal this very young part of us. In this way, we look to our partner to make us whole again.

Heartbreak is a very real consequence of an existence where we remain detached from our own source of vulnerability. When we have not invested in our own feelings of self-value and worth, we lean on our partner to give us these. However, relying on an external source for these feelings means that the pain of loss is felt all the more sharply when somebody pulls back from or leaves a relationship. The feelings that the relationship had been able to supply us with had a deeply impactful effect on us. We felt alive again. However, because we relied on somebody else for those affirmative feelings, we suffer the hugely painful consequences of abandonment and betrayal when the relationship is halted, our childhood wounds are reopened, everything about ourselves gets called into question as once again we ask, "Am I enough?"

This can trigger a whole sequence of events where our need for that particular supply of positive regard supersedes everything else. In a most sobering way we try and reclaim what we have lost, putting ourselves in very weak positions. This includes reaching out to somebody who has treated us with disregard or putting their needs before ours so we can continue to be part of the relationship. In other cases, we will let them go and when they suddenly bounce back into our lives, we step back into the relationship. Or we too easily give ourselves away by staying in weak relationships hoping that something will change and that we will finally be acknowledged properly. However, each time we do this, we lose a piece of ourselves again, re-wounding ourselves and confirming the belief that we are not good enough. In order to be regarded we need to play a particular role or be a *better* person. Sometimes we try to avoid the awful threat of rejection by adopting behaviours that we hope will make us acceptable or even indispensable. These behaviours further diminish our sense of value as we gradually drop our expectations of having our needs met. We begin to operate from a place of dependency, reinforcing the survival strategies that we learned as children when we sought approval from our parents. We present an idealised version of ourselves because we think the real version is not good enough.

By distancing ourselves from our vulnerability, we not only create barriers to emotionally connecting with ourselves, we obstruct the emotional pathway to connecting with others. When we disregard our true selves in this way, we sadly and tragically act from a place of self-judgment. We inadvertently hide our own truth and any relationship that we do form from this closed-off place of disconnection or pretence lacks true heartfelt presence and meaning.

Usually it takes a very significant life-changing event for us to finally begin to shed the protective shell that we created in childhood. This shell is made up of the beliefs, behaviours, and conditioning that we grew up with and which prevented us from honouring our emotions and feelings. These beliefs often had very negative connotations such as judgment, blame and shame, and there may have been little space for positive regard, value, and worth. In order to reconnect with our inner source of value, we need to go back to the time and place, when and where we lost it.

When we arrived in the world, we were inherently valuable. Our strengths and weakness do not in any way add to or detract from us. In fact, our strengths help us to survive in life and our weaknesses are our greatest teachers.

As already mentioned, we created habits, patterns, and beliefs in order to survive in the relational field of our family and our culture. As adults, when we do not allow ourselves the opportunity to interrogate or to dispel with these assumptions, we continue to engage in the same patterns of behaviour over and over again. Our task is to differentiate and separate from our childhood assumptions and life scripts that no longer serves us. When we turn away from this task, we continue to turn away from ourselves.

By using the process by which we lost our sight, we can reclaim it. Going back and reclaiming our vulnerability becomes the way in which we can integrate it and heal ourselves. This process lies at the heart of coming into wholeness; it is the mainstay of the *Self Centred Approach*.

Our imperfections represent the essence of our human nature. In turning towards them, we turn towards our humanity. Each time we acknowledge and listen to our true heartfelt self, we express our willingness to awaken to, and honour our authentic nature. This practice supports us in figuring out the parts that we lost, and when and where we lost them. By turning towards ourselves in this way, we can once again reconnect with the shadow parts that were deemed "unacceptable" in our families and our culture. For example, the part that felt exposed and shamed when it acted with exuberance and spontaneity. By quashing and dismissing these exuberant and spontaneous parts of our being, we unwittingly pushed hugely valuable energy that we need to live a fulfilling life, including our sense of wonder, spontaneity, creativity and playfulness, into our shadow. Carl Jung refers to this as "our golden shadow" because the wounded child part of us that we disconnected from is also the creative, playful, wondrous being full of awe—the dancing star within us. We rejected these parts or projected them onto others when it was not safe to hold them for ourselves; they shone too brightly for those around us. We continue to deny and repress these parts, holding them in our shadow until it is safe for them to emerge. Interestingly, these parts become ignited when we experience resentment towards others in whom we subconsciously recognise our repressed parts. For example, feelings of animosity towards the one who always gets her needs met signifies the emergence of a repressed or shadow part in us that was rejected or shamed when it sought to get its own needs met. When we recognise this part, we can bring it into consciousness and hold it. We can then integrate it by listening to it and giving it what it needs.

Reconnecting with our inner selves can enable us to reclaim these shadow parts. We can do this when we anchor ourselves internally by dropping down into our hearts. From this place of meaningful connection, we can bring a new compassion and understanding to our story. This means moving away from distrust and unworthiness, and towards inner trust and self-worth, where we get our needs met through true expression. In doing so, we also lift the barriers to connection with others in whom we recognise our shadow parts and we can replace these with a new understanding and empathy.

We can only become grounded in our humility, or what David Whyte calls *grounded humiliation*, and our true autonomous nature when we are integrated with our emotional source, our psychological source, and our physical source.

We each have an internal axis of reference, which is uniquely ours. It provides the opening through which we can inhabit our humility and move to a wholly integrated conscious state. This axis is made up of three reference points or three brains with complex neural pathways that are sources of intelligence, discernment and judgment:

Our head, the only part that is visible to the outside world, where we perceive information and process it.

Our heart, our emotional source of love and wisdom.

Our stomach, where our gut feelings come from. We feel butterflies when we are excited, anxiety when we are nervous, and nauseous when we are in shock.

These three brains combine to form our internal powerhouse and when connected, they represent the true foundation of who we are. So rather than just listening to stories in our heads, we can connect with a broader sense of being that has a much more grounded and meaningful base. Adopting the practice of breathing into and connecting with these reference points can become a rich way to ground ourselves. The minute we begin to honour our internal axis is the minute we begin to truly trust our own power. This can be facilitated through spiritual practices where, by staying in our breath, body, and cells, we can anchor ourselves and reconnect with our lost parts. When we connect with our heart, our source of wisdom and love, we can act from a place of compassion towards the vulnerable parts, which have experienced heartbreak, abandonment, hurt, and betrayal. From this inner connection with a very pure and authentic source of love, we can nurture feelings of inner value and worth. When we learn to trust our minds to process information we can speak from a place of self-belief. When we listen to our gut feeling, we bring our presence to whatever is unfolding. We can allow ourselves endless possibilities and step back from the paths that are not meant for us.

It is through this conscious awareness that we can hold our vulnerability and acknowledge the places where we hurt, whether it is fear, anxiety, shame, or any of the shadow parts we had to lose and disconnect from. When we do this, we connect in an intimate way with our true self, the part that is present when we are alone, the part that stays with us before we go to sleep at night and the part that is with us when we wake up in the morning.

When we act from this deeply honest and meaningful place, we no longer need to depend on external sources for feelings of value and worth, where unhealthy attachments, expectations, and the drama of our compulsions and addictions take centre stage. Instead we experience a sense of inner fulfilment, as our vulnerable parts can be acknowledged and included. In this place of presence, we can connect with and belong to ourselves. We begin to trust ourselves. In our knowing, judgment, and choices, we become steady. Conscious responses replace reactivity and insecurity as we very naturally and authentically empower ourselves to speak our truth and strive to achieve our aspirations. Consequently, our inclination towards uncomfortable negative thoughts and experiences is replaced by self-compassion and regard. We become attuned to the inner self and to the vulnerable self. We can acknowledge the critical voice and how it is trying to keep us small and safe and we can discard its messages if they no longer serve us.

It is only when we meet ourselves in a place of true compassion, that we can show compassion towards others. Then we can form relationships that are honest and meaningful and where we can be seen in our truth for who we really are.

Summary

We live in an imperfect world and we were brought up in an imperfect family, with its own idiosyncrasies and legacies. This is what it means to be fully human.

When we could not be seen for our inherent value, we learned how to seek positive regard in other ways. For each of us the strategy was different. When we needed to adapt to our family's value system, we unwittingly bought into certain belief systems about ourselves, and others. However, as adults, when we continue to act from this old tried and tested script, we continue to betray our true authentic and spontaneous nature. Thus, we can never truly be seen or belong, we can only be viewed for the roles that we step into in our relationships where we subconsciously create barriers to connecting in a *true-self-to-true-self* way, where two equals come together.

Moving towards our true self requires a kind of unlearning and letting go, where we may have to give up the construct that served us so well during our formative years. In order to reclaim the self that arrived in this world with an innate value, we need to allow our imperfections, our humility, and our true humanity to emerge. It is through acceptance and acknowledgement of this self that the process of growth can truly begin. Our vulnerability is the link through which we can reclaim this self.

When we enter an intimate relationship with another, we take responsibility for how we create and shape our space in the partnership. By looking at the behaviours, expectations, and performance standards that we adapt in our romantic relationships, we can understand the dynamics that we subconsciously engage in. Moving from reactive and confusing relationship dynamics to meaningful and responsive relationships, where we are seen and we belong, begins with self-compassion. In other words, we can first and foremost nurture and honour our self, and then our partner. The constructed self that we developed in childhood, which limits and confines us, can now be reconfigured and the inner self who represents our true integrity, vulnerability, and authentic energy can be integrated. From this place, we can live in a much larger and richer story. This is what the *Self Centred Approach* focuses on.

CHAPTER 6

THE PATHWAY TO LOVE

The minute I heard my first love story, I started looking for you, not knowing how blind that was.

Lovers don't finally meet somewhere.

They're in each other all along

Rumi

As Rumi's poem suggests our greatest source of love lies within each of us. This is also the argument for a *Self Centred Approach*. In the last chapter, we looked at the obstacles to self-compassion and love. I will now introduce you to new practices where we can begin to truly trust ourselves, and truly see and trust others.

We cultivate and nurture love when we allow our most vulnerable and powerful selves to be deeply seen and known. We succeed when we honour with trust, respect, kindness, and affection the spiritual connection and inner purpose that lives and grows within each of us. Usually it takes the pain of heartbreak for our hearts to be truly opened. For this reason, finding the pathway to love and belonging is one that is almost always punctuated with suffering; it is an inevitable consequence of our deeply caring and sincere humanity. Thus, we need to learn ways to open to and hold this pain.

When heartbreak arrives at our door, we very often blame ourselves, thinking we are somehow not enough or we are wrong. However, the truth is that without pain there is no opportunity for growth. The pain of heartbreak is a necessary pathway back to ourselves where we can experience who we truly are in this place of inner connection with the opened heart. It is a very important part of our journey, which needs to happen. It breaks the defensive shell that has up to this, held us in a small story about ourselves. The narrative of this story began in our childhood where we did not have the emotional resources to nurture a compassionate and self-valuing relationship with ourselves.

As already alluded to, we have each been conditioned in different ways by our families and larger culture. We adopted certain behaviours that would make us more acceptable at a time when we could not be appreciated for simply being ourselves. The self that we constructed in order to survive is referred to here as the false self. It enabled us to be more acceptable to our parents and adapt to cultural norms and expectations. This was a very necessary adaptation.

Our false self allows us to create a success system that appeals to the ego. It is the outer façade that is showcased to the world, often represented in social media by beautiful images that portray a curated lifestyle. Beneath this façade is an inner true self, in all its humanity. The mindfulness coach Kate James highlights the difference between the real and the false self when she exemplifies how we compare our inner selves to somebody else's exterior image or false self, depicted on social media. Even though we do not know what it is like to be them, that is, the person they meet when they close the door at night, we often harshly judge and compare our own self with the curated lifestyles of others. This has detrimental effects on our day-to-day lives where we experience anxiety, depression and "Fear Of Missing

Out (FOMO)", now a rapidly growing epidemic in our culture.

Our true self is our soul and our very life force. It was present in the heartbeat that heralded our presence to the world and it became the embodiment of who we are physically, sexually, emotionally and most of all spiritually. It is our authentic personality. The Buddhist psychologist and teacher Tara Brach refers to the true self as the part that keeps us grounded, allowing us to be truly present, open, and courageous.

The process of learning to connect with and inhabit our vulnerability sets the stage for us to reconnect with the star that we entered the world with, that is our authentic energy, the place where we are most present and connected with our true self. The big question is, do we want to grow and edge closer to a place of intimate connection with ourselves, or do we choose to continue with the same relationship patterns in the hope that next time the outcome will be different?

When we choose to grow, we allow a conscious space to open up where we afford ourselves the opportunity to:

Observe and witness the behaviours that we adopt when we are in relationships.

Begin to understand the parts that prevent us from achieving fulfilling relationships where we are seen, valued, and belong.

Creating this space allows us to revisit the place where we first learned how to relate in an intimate space. This was the relationship we experienced as young children with our parents. By re-inhabiting this space, we can understand and unravel the rationale behind our expectations, performance standards, and the relationship dynamics that we continue to automatically engage with. Our mature selves can now bring compassion to these very young places where we still get hooked and caught up in roles and behaviours that no longer serve our highest good. Through this compassionate presence, we can allow ourselves to discern the parts that serve our best interests as adults, and those that do not. To facilitate this, it is important to understand the now out of date and misinformed place that these parts continue to act from. It enables us to identify and make conscious our old programme so we can update it and integrate new self-regarding, self-valuing, and self-fulfilling practices. The place I am referring to here is our old brain.

As mentioned earlier, we each have a primitive old brain that is wired to a fear response. It is grounded in our evolution where it was critical to our survival to perceive danger in a world inhabited by poisonous snakes and plants, tigers, lions and other threats to our physical safety. This fear response is intrinsic to our self-protection. Over the millennia it has become so deeply wired in our brains that when we are in real danger, it is automatically triggered. However, sometimes our fear response becomes prevalent in our everyday lives, where we automatically link past experiences with current circumstances. For example, when we do not get the response we had hoped for our mind automatically perceives rejection or abandonment and we move into protective structures. Mentally we become distracted, we rehearse what we are going to say and how we are going to act. Emotionally we are overtaken with uncomfortable and insecure feelings; behaviourally we act from a place that seeks to illicit a particular response—sometimes our nervous system response takes over and we attack or defend. Consequently we are no longer grounded in our humility where our emotional and feeling sense is present and spontaneous. We become disconnected from our true self, and we get caught in behaviours that are driven by fear of abandonment and rejection. In short, we abandon ourselves and we act from our false self where:

We seek validation from others, instead of self-regarding and self-valuing.

We portray ourselves in a scripted way where we only show the parts that we think will be regarded. We withhold our true heartfelt, emotional experience, keeping ourselves unseen.

We comply with other peoples' belief systems, putting our own to the side.

We act from a place of reactivity and fear as opposed to presence and spontaneity.

We may even accept culpability when another blames, shames, or judges us.

The false self, whom we adopted in our childhood, automatically shows up again when we enter intimate relationships where, just like riding a bicycle, we automatically fall into a familiar pattern of behaviour. In this dynamic we identify with our false self, taking it to be who we are, and our true, authentic self becomes hijacked. However, when we automatically adopt very young beliefs and behaviours in our adult relationships, we act against ourselves. So when our partner blames or judges us, our false self either believes the shaming and reacts by self-blaming, or it gets into a defensive position and reacts by shutting down emotionally.

Creating a conscious space to identify and understand our emotions when we find ourselves in challenging situations is central to the *Self Centred Approach* introduced, in terms of the quality of the relationship that we develop with ourselves, and with others. Our ability to remain present and aware, as opposed to reactive and defensive, greatly influences the level of trust we can establish with ourselves and with others. By recognising unhealthy and unsupportive behaviours for what they really are, we prevent ourselves from getting triggered and hooked into the unconscious trance of our old brain's survival mode. So when control, judgment, blame, or resentment show up, we can observe them from a place of presence and connection, without falling victim to the false self, who learned to automatically comply with or react to these behaviours. By seeking to understand our emotions, we stay on the pathway to love.

The contemporary thought leader Panache Desai describes emotions as energies in motion. For every emotion, there is a feeling. By acknowledging our uncomfortable emotions and identifying the feelings behind them, we stand a greater chance of processing them and integrating them. As Dr. Daniel Siegel states, "by naming them we tame them." The naming shifts us to the new brain, the *neocortex*. Therefore, when we experience frustration and anger, we can connect with our true selves where our vulnerability stems from, and identify the feelings behind our emotions. For example, behind the armour of anger and frustration, often feelings of hurt and abandonment can be revealed. From this place of inner connection, we can hold and soothe the part that is hurting with compassion. This is what creating a conscious space means. It is critical to developing a nurturing relationship with our self, and with others. This is how our emotions can be processed and integrated into a more whole self.

Our internal dialogue and processes are subconsciously reflected in our outward behaviour and actions. When we do not process our emotions, not only do we treat ourselves harshly, but we also transfer our emotions in a toxic way to others in passive-aggressive or avoidant behaviour. Therefore, when we give authority to the voice of our inner *critic*, we not only self-criticise, we also project these feelings onto others, and we criticise them. However, as soon as we identify the *critic*, we create a space to understand its motivation. For example, we can connect with the unseen or disappointed part of us, where this voice stems from, and nurture it with kindness and understanding. By doing this, a softening can occur where we can transform our feelings, freeing ourselves from the experience of being overwhelmed by them or subject to them. Adopting this process enables us to act from a place of emotional connection as opposed to a cut-off defensive place, activated by our nervous system.

What we feel on the inside is portrayed on the outside, in our thoughts, feelings, and actions. When we act from a place of inner connection, we can enter relationships in an emotionally present way and it is also likely that we will attract an emotionally viable relationship. Contrastingly, when we operate from a cut-off place, detached from our emotions, we can engage in the physical and psychological aspects of the relationship, and remain separated from any emotional connection.

By taking a closer look at why we find it so hard to trust and regard our true authentic nature, and why we so easily turn the finger of blame in our own direction when things go wrong, we can open to the really important, positive, and meaningful aspects of our true self. This opening can be supported by a new awareness about how we perceive and process responses and feedback from others. Understanding our negative bias, also known as the negativity effect, can facilitate us in doing this.

As mentioned earlier, as part of our evolution we developed strategies, which focused on identifying threats to our survival. This means that our nervous system is wired into seeing and perceiving negativity or threats over positivity and neutrality. As a result, our old brain clings to things of a negative nature even when positive or neutral thoughts are present in equal intensity. Each time we replay stories about negative situations, we give energy to our negative bias and we activate the old part of our brain that is wired to survival and protective strategies. When this happens, our bodies become flooded with cortisol, the stress hormone and our *flight, fight*, or *freeze* nervous system response is triggered.

Our psychological state is more affected by negative as opposed to neutral or positive experiences. By learning to regulate the negative bias, which is hardwired into our brains, we can come into presence with our authentic nature. Roy Baumeister, a world-renowned social psychologist, attests that negative experiences are more than two times more powerful than positive ones. New neuroscience suggests that this figure is as high as five times. When we do not take time to experience and process the negative and disturbing feelings that overshadow us, they affect us in powerful ways, which become part of our life. So when we repeatedly pay attention to and believe the stories of shame and judgment, we believe them to be true. We further strengthen the negative bias when we create a habit of continuously perpetuating the behaviours that stem from a place of low self-worth.

Our attitudes and approaches to relationships are governed by these false emotions, which we are held hostage by, and which appear real to us, for example:

"I am not good enough."

"I will never be regarded for who I truly am."

"When I express my true feelings, I will be knocked back and rejected."

"I need to live in a false self of pretence in order to be accepted and noticed."

"I am not important, I always need to put everyone else first."

"I will only be noticed when I serve others."

"Even when others disregard me, I will still seek their approval when they show up again."

"I need to seek validation in order to feel a sense of OK-ness."

As long as we live in and identify with a restrictive and punitive story about ourselves, we remain merged to the story. We believe it represents the truth, taking it to be who we are. So when the story stems from the child who was abandoned or betrayed, we become identified with the one who is abandoned or betrayed. Consequently we can never come into presence because there is no conscious space to witness this as the story that it is. When we live in this limited story, we attract others from this place.

However, when we create a conscious space for holding and inquiring into these beliefs, we afford ourselves the opportunity to interrogate the story, and to experience and process the feelings that hold us back. The more we create a compassionate space to see the negative bias, the more it loosens its grip on us and relinquishes its control over us.

We each have our own unique expression of energy, which feeds into the vibrational field in which we connect to others. When we nurture inner compassion, we practice self-acceptance and inner regard. Once we connect with our own unique purpose, we can value ourselves and become our own leader. From this place of inner regard we can empower ourselves to consider:

What if I choose to live in a truer version of myself and bring to the relationship who I really am and stop judging myself for who I think I *should* be?

What if I choose to honour my purpose, speak my truth, and no longer depend on others' responses for approval?

What if I choose to regard myself and choose to no longer engage with those who do not regard me for who I am?

One of the biggest reasons we stay stuck in old mind-sets is FEAR, which can be held as an acronym for False Evidence Appearing Real. Fear acts to restrict us to certain behaviours and it limits our freedom to pursue what we truly desire. When fear controls us, we limit our expectations and belief systems about ourselves, separating from any possibility of living a wholehearted and fully present life. From this *safe* place, it is easier to act with impulses, ruled by old beliefs that tell us how we *should* and *need* to behave as opposed to how we *want* or *choose* to. When we live in this way, we deprive ourselves of true joy and fulfilment.

Fear connects us to the old brain and our *flight, fight,* or *freeze* protective response mechanism. It disconnects us from who we really are in the present moment, in our adult state. In other words, fear holds us back and keeps us small. When fear enters our relationships, we behave in certain restrictive ways, for example, we seek approval, afraid that if we honour who we really are, we will be rejected, chastised, and shamed.

What if we were to challenge that fear and say, "No more!"

What would happen if we no longer allowed these false emotions to influence our lives?

What if we realised that there was no truth or foundation to the restrictive voices that we listen to?

What if we were to bring a new intention to our behaviour that allowed us to free ourselves from fear?

Our false self is motivated by fear, whereas our true self is motivated by love and regard for who we are. We continue to act in cycles of fear when we are unwilling to inquire into it and become aware of what drives it. In order to free ourselves from this self-limiting behaviour, we must look inward and acknowledge the voice that drives it—this is an act of self-love. When we consciously create a space to inquire into our true feelings, then we can practice taking small risks. More importantly, we can consider what the consequences will be if we do not take these risks.

The biggest obstacle in our way is always fear. What we rarely stop to consider is the degree to which we deprive ourselves from true fulfilment when we allow it to rule our relationships. When we do not confront our fear, we continue to act from a place of powerlessness, sabotaging our ability to experience true joy.

Deepak Chopra states that,

> *Words build relationships and we are*
> *the authors of our own story.*

The most important relationship of all is the one we have with ourselves. When we speak truthfully, we speak with self-regard and when we nurture feelings of inner compassion and love, we can move closer to a position of inner empowerment and strength. By changing our internal dialogue, we can shift from a place of fear and uncertainty to confidence and achievement. For example, by replacing:

"If only" with "I will"

"I cannot" with "I have bravery and strength within me that I do not know about"

"I'm fine" with "I'm struggling with something"

"I should" with "I want to"

"I'm not enough" with "I'm more than enough"

"I do not have enough" with "I am wealthy, I have all the passion and energy I need to support me in living the life I want"

"I'll never get what I want" with "New opportunities will open up to me when I channel my energy towards them"

"It is too hard" with "All the strength and support I need will be there for me when I need it"

Every time we speak with compassion and understanding to ourselves and to others, we see the world as a place where we can trust ourselves, and where we experience the world as trustworthy. When we practise behaviour that represents such self-belief, we act from an intention that is based on possibility. As Gary Zukav says:

> *Every action, thought, and feeling is motivated by an intention, and that intention is a cause that exists as one with an effect. If we participate in the cause, it is*

not possible for us not to participate in the effect.
In this most profound way we are held responsible
for our every action, thought, and feeling,
which is to say, for our every intention.

Our intention dictates how we live our life and what we get out of it. We consciously create our reality with the intention we choose to live by. In other words, the choices we make, the energy, passion and sense of purpose we invest in our everyday lives create the blueprint for our future. The question we need to ask ourselves is, do we choose to act from a place of love or fear? By interrogating and challenging the self-defeating stories that we subconsciously tell ourselves about ourselves, we act from a place of self-compassion and love. Each time we do this, we soothe the frightened inner child—this is a pathway to love.

For each of us the intention is different. For example, by acting from a place of fear, our intention might be to invest our energy in seeking approval from others. This results in placing ourselves in a position of weakness where we subconsciously rely on others' terms of acceptance, not our own. When the cause is to act with love and compassion for our true selves, the effect is joy, inner power, and inner fulfilment.

When we practise consciousness and go inside to our internal place of being, we can connect with our heart space and authentic energy. In this place of connection, we can hold an intention based on love and endless possibility. We can nurture this intention by actively pursuing habits that support it and becoming aware of the things that rob us from it. For example, when comparison, resentment, and judgment show up, we can be sure that these are coming from the false self. By recognising this, we can consciously look inward and meet these feelings with compassion and understanding. The more we cultivate love, the more we provide a holding environment for our true selves to grow and develop.

The moment we begin to live from a place of intention that is aligned with a truer version of ourselves, is the moment we start harnessing a life filled with meaning and joy, where endless possibilities abide. This means becoming aware of the self-destructive cycles of behaviour and stories that sabotage our inner freedom and power, creating loving and joyful consequences for our future. So when we enter relationships, we can have a more objective and a more mature outlook. This means holding ourselves accountable and staying true to our intention and purpose. If our intention is to have a mutually supportive, committed relationship, we can express this at the beginning of a relationship. In doing so, we regard our intention, putting ourselves in a position of strength where we give our partner the opportunity to respond. By allowing ourselves to discern the behavioural patterns that are aligned to our intention, we endeavour to give to ourselves what our heart truly desires. In this way, we stay in full balance with the true feelings that lie behind our experiences, aligning ourselves with who we are and what we represent.

Affirmations can provide the link to this transformative process. New research in neuroscience demonstrates that affirmations can connect us with the new brain that can take a bigger perspective and counteract the old brain's fear and negative bias. So when we say, "I love you, you are more than enough, you deserve to have a supportive relationship where you are seen, you are regarded and you belong," we soothe the part that self-doubts. Similarly, when we focus on the negative by saying, "I am not enough," we trigger old brain responses of fear and catastrophe, highlighting the part that makes us suffer. When we nurture the voice that speaks from the heart, we can bring ourselves closer to the star that we each arrived in this world with. The more we allow our compassionate voice to speak, the more we strengthen it. Thus, when our negative bias is activated, we can acknowledge it for the anxious, frightened, and usually much younger part of ourselves that it represents. We can soothe and nurture it with compassion and understanding, no longer allowing the judge and critic to have free rein by shaming our vulnerable part and moving it into the shadow again.

Through this process we can break free from self-limiting beliefs and behaviours and begin to act from a place of self-compassion, where we are willing to take ownership of our own worth. In doing this, we unlock our truth and set ourselves free to live life in harmony and honour our true selves. This has profound consequence for how we experience ourselves in relationships and how we are in the world at large.

We arrived in this world with our own unique star. We are drawn closer to it when we inhabit a place where self-compassion, kindness and inner love can dwell, and where we recognise and become grateful for the beauty that lies within us. When we allow beauty to enter our world, be it is the splendour of nature, the goodness that we recognise in others, or the compassion and empathy we experience when we see suffering, we emulate the thoughts and feelings that we experience. When we focus on kindness and vulnerability, that is what we project to the world.

As our level of consciousness deepens, we become intuitively aware when we need to realign with our true selves, we can do this through the breath, stillness, or silence. Other practices that can enable us to stay on the pathway to love include meditation, journaling, yoga, massage, music, dance or being in nature. Through the breath, we can focus on the internal space that connects our three brains: our heart, our mind, and our gut.

Summary

When life is such that we are pulled in different directions by the pressures of an ever-evolving world with all its real, virtual, or imaginary distractions, it is not always possible to live in the here-and-now. We can so easily lose our selves in stories, comparisons, and judgment, which only serve to create distance and barriers from connecting with our true self.

We can change our out-dated childhood programme by developing new conscious practices that bring us back into alignment with our humility, our vulnerability, and our true humanity. These practices are based on self-seeing, self-regarding, and self-valuing. This requires a letting go and unlearning of old behaviours that are deeply ingrained in us. The performance standards and beliefs about ourselves that we adopted as children can now be identified for the survival strategies that they represented when it was not possible for our true selves to be accepted and seen.

By making a commitment to align with our true selves, we put in place a protective system that acts to protect, regard, and serve our most precious, sacred, rich and true source of love. When we do this, we set an intention to honour who we are and what our heart truly desires, choosing to live more freely, joyfully, powerfully, and compassionately. We now have the permission to pursue new behaviours and practices where we can act with compassion towards ourselves. We embed these each time we bring into consciousness our automatic reactions and give ourselves permission to respond from a place of here-and-now feelings and emotions. This means undertaking new behaviours and new ways of relating in our relationships where we not only see ourselves honestly, but we allow others to see us in the same way. This is true maturity–this is the true pathway to love.

CHAPTER 7

REDEFINING INTIMACY

Love is not something we give or get; it is something
that we nurture and grow, a connection can only
be cultivated between two people when it exists
within each one of them, we can only love others
as much as we love ourselves.

Brené Brown

Brené Brown states that in order for love to enter a relationship with another, it needs to exist within us first. Love is not
something that is automatically acquired, rather, we allow it
to enter when we take what Mark Nepo calls the "exquisite
risk" of choosing to stay present and honour our true feelings. It is through this wholehearted presence that we can

harness love with understanding and care. As discussed in the last chapter, the pathway to love comes with true maturity where we can become consciously aware of our protective or defensive parts that no longer serve us, and instead regard our frightened and wounded parts with care and attention. We have the capacity to hold and to honour these vulnerable parts within the container of a compassionate self.

When our only reference point for intimacy is the behaviour we adopted in order to survive in the family we grew up in, we find it hard to learn and apply new behaviours that support us in opening to an intimate space. However, now we can adopt a new reference point of internal nurturing where we can treat with care and understanding our wounded parts when they emerge. These include the parts that experience feelings of "not good enough" when we perceive we are being judged. By fostering our compassionate voice we begin to grow and develop the internal parent, who can hold and nurture our wounded parts and not allow our inner judge to criticize or shame them when we make mistakes. In this way, we can bring our wounded parts into alignment with who we are in our relationships, where we can then remain present and connected, no longer needing to run from our vulnerability.

I define intimacy as, "a *true-self-to-true-self* way of relating, where we can be in our most grounded, connected and vulnerable state with another, free from roles and expectations dominated by gender or culture." Intimacy really means In To Me See, which is only possible when we are in tune with our inner world. Hence, when we can allow our self to act from a place of wholeheartedness, where our wounded parts can also be acknowledged and held with compassion, we allow a space to open up where a meaningful connection with another can take place. For this reason, the *Self Centred Approach* invites us to reach a level of maturity that includes self-seeing, self-compassion, and honesty with ourselves, so that we can accept with love and understanding the truth of who we really are, not a romanticized version of who we think we are, or an idealized self that we think somebody else expects us to be. When we truly accept ourselves, we can allow another to truly see us. When we quash our vulnerable parts, we inadvertently act to obstruct intimacy. We subconsciously adopt a *detached approach* to our relationships, where we detach from our vulnerability and humility, we play a particular role that we perceive as acceptable or desirable, and we shy away from the exquisite risk of exposing our true nature.

When we can learn the practice of regarding our humanity, we can then communicate with others from a very real place. Carl Rogers uses the term congruence to describe when the internal self and the idealized self are in alignment with each other. We lack congruence when we act out of an idealized mask and we keep our true self hidden.

As explored in the last chapter, when we place our self at the heart of the approach that we take to attracting an intimate relationship, we greatly increase our chances of successfully achieving a *true-self-to-true-self* connection, where our authenticity and imperfect humanity can be regarded. Conversely, when we consider a *detached approach* to attracting a relationship, where we present our outer shell to the world, we focus on the superficial aspects of a relationship. By setting the stage in this way, we live out of the false self, which includes idealisations, projections, and rejections. Here the superficial aspects of the relationship will stay at the forefront and a true connection will remain out of reach.

In addition to this, we implicitly give a message to our wounded inner child that she is not acceptable. This has an additional wounding effect on the child who is not welcome in the relationship. As a consequence, she goes underground where she has to work much harder to get her needs met. In her fierceness to do this, she sabotages the relationship through manipulations such as passive-aggressive and attention-seeking behaviours. By rejecting our inner wounded child, we fail to live out of a true version of ourselves. The *Self Centred Approach* is asking us to take the exquisite risk of being true to all our different parts, including our lost parts. We do this when we allow ourselves the freedom of wholehearted presence, where we can remain connected with our humility and vulnerability. Subsequently, our potential for enjoyment and connection greatly increases. This has a very positive feedback effect where we exude a sense of true presence, which attracts others. When we allow our true self to govern how we engage and interact with others, our experience of the relationship becomes very significant. This means that:

We operate from a very real, grounded place, which includes honesty and imperfection.

We act with self-regard and awareness for our internal experience.

We remain in our wholeness, our relationships are wholehearted and our experience is very meaningful.

By self-accepting and self-regarding, we do not seek acceptance and regard from the other.

We can be present, spontaneous, and responsive in the moment, rather than caught up in a story of how the relationship should unfold. This greatly enhances our experience of the moment, where:

We exude a sense of inner presence and vitality.

We act with purposeful energy as opposed to remaining passive, in the hope that things will work out.

Therefore, in order to attract a high-quality responsive relationship, there are two really important factors that we need to consider:

We need to be in our self and hold our integral energy, meaning that we stay attuned to our inner world, where we make conscious and hold with compassion all our parts. From this place we can regard and trust ourselves.

We need to have the emotional flexibility that allows us to grow.

Our desire to experience a deep and meaningful connection with another can trigger our willingness to grow. This opens us up to parts that previously we have not been able to experience, including new levels of emotional vulnerability. This inner growth is based on a deep and meaningful connection to self. Our capacity for intimate connection depends on our ability to operate from a place of conscious awareness and acceptance, as opposed to a place of defence or denial. So when we experience discomfort or feelings of "not good enough," we can recognise this very young part and acknowledge it by saying,

> *"I know you are hurting, I can see you,*
> *and I understand. You are truly loved and you*
> *are truly valuable."*

In this way, we go to a place of compassion, which allows us to stay connected to our internal experience instead of running from it. This is not done in a way where we try to convince ourselves, but rather, a way where we connect with our heart and from this place of warmth and compassion, we soothe our very young, vulnerable parts with tenderness and love. When we allow our compassionate voice to speak and be heard, we seek to truly see ourselves. As we develop the practice of staying with and holding our vulnerability in this way, the wounded child within us can relax its hold on us, and be more at ease. In this way, the child knows that it is welcome, it has its place, therefore, it is no longer tightly grabbing onto us. Through this practice of wholehearted presence, we begin to allow ourselves to be seen by others. This is what it means to develop an intimate connection. Importantly, when we can connect with ourselves honestly, we can act from a base of confidence and we can grow.

Thus, as we learn to use our internal nourishing and soothing voice to reassure, we subsequently open up the pathway for intimacy to grow with another. In order to nurture this intimate connection, it is important that we continue to pay attention to our own internal relationship, and our often subconscious behavioural patterns.

In the *Self Centred Approach* I am arguing that we need to take care of the little one ourselves and we do not bring that need into the relationship. When unconscious expectations enter a relationship, they create barriers, which take away from our ability to develop an intimate and trusted connection. In the *Self Centred Approach* it is our place to take care of ourselves, to see ourselves, to own our own feelings and to take responsibility for expressing our needs.-

We create a sacred space where a relationship can grow and develop without restriction when our innermost thoughts and feelings can be expressed and met with support and regard. For example when we share with our partner our experience of:

Hurt and disappointment when we perceive we are not considered or regarded properly.

Love and regard when we are considered, appreciated, and valued.

This practice of connecting with our feelings and then expressing them in a wholehearted way requires us to turn away from habit, automatic reactions and roles. Instead, we give ourselves the space to respond in a present way to our interactions and emotional experiences as they unfold. In this way, we connect with our vulnerability. By responding from this place, we nurture an emotional connection in our relationships and we allow ourselves to be truly seen (In To Me See). When we dismiss, without question, uncomfortable, or difficult experiences in our relationships, we dismiss our needs and they remain unseen.

Moreover, by communicating our experience from a place of connection with our vulnerability, we help our partner to understand our needs and to see into us more. We also create the opportunity for our partner to respond. This is true maturity and intimacy in action. This also allows our partner the opportunity to express his or her desires. Creating a space for compassionate communication to take place provides an opportunity to grow and develop a vital sense of awareness in the relationship. This act of true expression ultimately serves to deepen the connection.

When we are too afraid to risk exposing our vulnerability and finding out if our partner will see us, meet us, and respond to us with understanding and regard, we can sit in the silence of disappointment, resentment, or withdrawal. The *Self Centred Approach* is predicated on nurturing our internal emotional resources where we self-see and self-regard. This is only possible when we connect with our humility and vulnerability because these are the sources of our greatest emotional strength, where we experience feelings of steadiness, and we grow in confidence. From this place of grounding we can empower ourselves to take the risk of finding out if the other can meet us. This is how we show up for ourselves, how we regard and value our experience, and how we allow ourselves to be seen.

When we do not express our true feelings, we remain unseen and very soon our old, unconscious *reptilian* brain hijacks the conscious, perspective-taking, and intention-making *neocortex* that supports us in making decisions and staying in alignment with these decisions. Our *reptilian* brain puts us into defence mode, where we become disconnected from our source of compassion and love; and where new polarities of *less than* and *better than* enter the dynamic. As a result, our connection with the other becomes severed.

So how can we stay present, steady and develop true intimacy in the face of uncomfortable feelings and difficult experiences as they emerge in our relationships?

The Self Centred Approach upholds that in learning the practice of staying with being vulnerable, we learn to hold our vulnerable feelings and become curious about them. So when our vulnerability is unexpectedly triggered we do not become overwhelmed by our feelings and go offline. This practice enables us to we develop new neural pathways that support us in staying conscious and connected internally, so that we can stay present, grounded, and steady, without going into story or taking up defensive stances when uncomfortable feelings are triggered.

By bringing a sense of purpose to how we experience our relationships, we give ourselves permission to remain open to new behaviours and responses. Rather than automatically stepping into roles and trying to fulfil perceived expectations, we step back and consciously observe as the relationship unfolds. This is a necessary practice that we need to adopt in order to remain open and responsive to the hugely meaningful and often inexplicable mystery that accompanies true intimacy.

When we practise presence, we can begin to link our behaviours as adults with the child who adopted these behaviours in order to survive. In opening our eyes to our automatic relationship adaptations, we can bring into consciousness the protective systems we used at a time when our star was too bright for those around us and we could not live out of our true selves. This explains why we still believe that if the true version of ourselves speaks with honesty, we will be rejected. Consequently we experience huge frustration, as we continue to live in a story which focuses on the daughter or son who seeks to be seen. Whether it is the daughter who thinks she needs to put her father's needs first, or the son who thinks he needs to be strong and not express his feelings, we continue to subconsciously employ these survival strategies in our intimate relationships.

When we allow this very young part to take centre stage, we stay stuck in old childhood injunctions where we still believe we need to be vigilant in this intimate space, where wounds of shame and self-judgment will re-emerge if we are not.

Childhood experiences of abandonment, dismissal, rejection, or betrayal have a deeply wounding effect. However, when we can acknowledge, hold, and reassure our very young wounded parts with love and compassion, we begin the process of giving these parts the attention they so desperately seek. Connecting with a supportive other, such as a therapist, when we experience painful feelings can further support us in being compassionately seen, held, and understood. Through the pure and raw expression of our feelings, we allow our wounds to be held, nurtured, and healed. In this way, we develop the internal nurturing mother who can meet the needs of her wounded child. From this place of inner nurturing and compassion, we begin to build our emotional support structure, which holds, soothes, and heals our vulnerable parts when they emerge. This provides the starting point for true intimacy to grow in our relationship with our self.

Like all beginners on a new journey, we will encounter struggles as the constructed self that we have worked so vigilantly to hold onto is asked to loosen its grip. As we grow to trust our journey, we begin to lower our protective layer and a new ease can emerge as we come to appreciate the huge amount of effort required to hold our constructed self in place. We do not have to fully give up the constructed self. We may still need it when we need to go into performance mode in some way. We just need to be watchful that it does not become us.

As long as we continue to shy away from the exquisite risk of honouring our true nature, expressing our true feelings and regarding our experience, we continue to avoid intimacy, and we risk re-wounding ourselves over and over again.

It is very likely that up to this point, without the insight to understand and trust our thoughts and feelings when they emerged in our relationships, it simply was not possible to truly and honestly allow ourselves to be seen. Bringing our childhood perceptions about ourselves and about our partner into awareness supports us in no longer stepping into a relationship with another *father* or *mother* role in order to heal our wounded child. By growing our own internal nurturing Mother, we can provide this healing environment for ourselves. This frees us to stay in our adult selves where we remain steady and grounded. From this place, we can empower ourselves and discern how we engage in our relationships. We evidence this to ourselves when we no longer need to seek the approval of Mother's or Father's gaze in this intimate sphere. With each new step we take on our journey towards intimacy, we grant ourselves more and more freedom to follow our passion and achieve meaningful experiences in our relationships.

Summary

The quality of our relationships is hugely dependent on how we protect, nurture, and care for them. This means caring for the space that we inhabit within our relationships. In this sense, truly caring means truly meeting ourselves, and truly meeting our partner. When we connect with our humility, we stay grounded and confident. From this openhearted and compassionate place, we allow an intimate space to grow where we can be seen and we can see our partner; we create a new way of relating, free from roles and expectations.

Very often the tendency in relationships is to become stuck in a groove of "your roles" and "mine." Intimacy is a *true-self-to-true-self* way of relating, not a gendered or cultured way. However, when we think the role of the other is to service the needs of me, needing them to give me X or Y, we stop seeing them for the person we were first attracted and drawn to and instead, we operate from a place where roles take centre stage.

Each time we develop the practice of acknowledging our internal experience and holding it with compassion and understanding, we nurture our internal soothing Mother.

When we self-see and regard ourselves, we enable ourselves to understand our experience. When we express our experience to our partner, we take the exquisite risk of allowing ourselves to be seen. It is in this place of connection that we develop and grow in our relationships.

When we bring a sense of purpose to how we experience our relationships, we allow ourselves to acknowledge our constructed selves, and then we can let go of them. By staying present, we open ourselves up to new possibilities and new outcomes. The ability to stay present is facilitated by the practice of holding and nurturing our wounded inner child when she or he shows up in this intimate relational sphere. Through recognising and then nourishing this very young part of us, we heal our inner child. This is how we set her or him free. Subsequently, we are able to step into our adult selves where we can remain open to each new, mysterious, and hugely meaningful experience as it emerges in this intimate sphere.

CHAPTER 8

LOVE, DESIRE, AND EROTICISM

Love enjoys knowing everything about you; desire
needs mystery. Love likes to shrink the distance
that exists between me and you, while desire
is energized by it. If intimacy grows through
repetition and familiarity, eroticism is numbered
by repetition. It thrives on the mysterious, the
novel, and the unexpected. Love is about having;
desire is about wanting.

Esther Perel

Up to this point, I have been talking about the pathway
to love, which brings us to a place of connection with our
whole self. In the erotic sphere, this becomes very important

because in order to have a *whole-self-to-whole-self* connection with another, we need space to nurture the relationship with our self separately, where we can become whole, mysterious, and spontaneous. When we give too much of ourselves to another, we lose our sense of self. The renowned author and psychotherapist Esther Perel believes that eroticism needs mystery. It requires presence and openness in order to go into the unknown with the other. Desire can only be nurtured and energized when we protect our autonomy or sense of self-governing, and eroticism requires a coming together of two individual whole selves in order to create the vital and visceral energy that the union creates. A *Self Centred Approach* to relationships requires us to be selfish, where we stay attuned with our inner world and, most importantly, we meet our partner in that space. In order for the erotic sphere of the relationship to become enlivened, two whole awakened selves must come together and share an integral source of energy which fuels and enlivens the union. Conversely, when we do not allow ourselves the freedom to act with our own agency, we act from the false self or the empty shell of our being and we rely on the energy of the other, or vice versa. In order to understand the importance of our autonomy in the erotic sphere, let us begin by taking a look at the meaning of desire and eroticism.

Desire is defined as a strong feeling of wanting to have something or wishing for something to happen. It is the force that drives attraction. The word desire comes from the Latin word *desiderare*, meaning "away from your star." It represents the feeling of longing experienced when we sense that we are separate from what we love. Desire draws us back to the energy and love that is our true source of energy; we arrived in the world with it. In this sense, desire and eroticism go hand in hand. Eroticism means life energy. It is derived from the Greek god, Eros, who celebrates the love of life. The ancient Greeks referred to Eros' energy as wild, passionate, fiery, and fierce. Erotic energy has a profound visceral and sensual quality to feeling and experiencing pleasure and excitement. It is driven by an unencumbered and raw life force, which can only be possible when we are fully present as our whole selves. When desire and eroticism come together, the part of us that yearns to be connected with our source of energy and love, and the part that is driven by the fierce and raw energy that represents our instinct for life, merge in an experience that resonates in the most vital, instinctive, reaffirming, and reawakening way.

However, while we try to capture the essence of desire and eroticism in our relationships, we often misunderstand the fundamental characteristics that are required to sustain an erotic connection. This misconception can be explained when we contrast the qualities that we understand to represent a stable intimate relationship, such as dependability, predictability, and belonging with the qualities that are necessary in order to access our erotic source which include distance, longing, and independence. What we think will bring us closer together with our partner acts instead to create barriers to connecting in the most visceral way. So when the unconscious contract that we create with another implies that we forsake our own desires, passions, and wants, in order to satisfy the needs of our partner, we disconnect from very vital parts of our being, and vice versa.

Hence, in order to nurture eroticism in our relationships we need to protect our autonomy, agency, and desire. This has been the main argument for the *Self Centred Approach* where we, first and foremost, create a space where we can be *Self Centred* and present with our whole selves before we can be present to another.

Esther Perel attests that desire is held in the space where we connect with our inner selves, the source of our true sensuality where we can evoke feelings of love and long-ing, excitement and sensations. I am saying that in order to evoke these feelings we need to allow and welcome our child self who is a very sensual, playful, spontaneous, imaginative, and erotic being. Thus, by creating a conscious space to con-nect with our inner child, we can be present with all these wondrous parts. For this connection to be made possible, a disconnection from the everyday pressures and responsibili-ties of life must be permitted because true presence can only be made possible in a space unburdened by any roles, labels, or expectations. It is in this space of inner connection, unen-cumbered by our protective parts and responsibilities, that we enable the other to see us, and vice versa.

As discussed in the last chapter, we cultivate our inner presence each time we experience our thoughts and feelings from a place of consciousness. When we do this, we gift to ourselves the opportunity to grow and move closer to our edge as multidimensional mysterious beings. Significantly, when we create a space where we can nurture our own source of innate energy and mystery, we no longer become enmeshed in that of others. Instead, we access the portal to our sensu-ality. We express this in our eyes, in our hearts, in how we listen, touch, and act. It is from this place of inner presence, that we instinctively attract our partner. Subsequently, the field of erotic energy becomes enlivened, as two whole inner selves express themselves in a very unique, pure, and vital way. The mirroring that we experience when we look into our partner's eyes from this place of presence enables us to experience feelings of radiance and vitality that have become enlivened by the connection.

The energy force of desire and eroticism is so powerful and magnetic, that in order to experience it, certain sequences, events, and consequences are required. The author Jack Morrin asserts that attraction plus obstacles equals excitement. In his book *The Erotic Mind*, he describes "longing and anticipation" as one of the cornerstones of eroticism. The quality of longing that embodies desire is something that we can experience only from a distance. Absence fosters feelings of yearning and longing for our lover and excitement and anticipation for what is to come when we are reunited. When we create an environment that is completely separate from the banal aspects of life, including all the things that distract us from the present moment, we can create an opening where we can reconnect with our inner self and meet our partner in a sensual way.

When we disconnect from our inner presence, the source of our true essence and vitality, which attracted our partner to us in the first place, becomes deadened. Instead, we operate from an automatic place, no longer attuned to our true nature. This happens when:

We lose ourselves either in a job, a relationship, our family, or whatever it is that takes us away from our selves.

Over reliance, expectation and dependence creep into our relationships.

Constancy replaces adventure and excitement.

Security replaces the anticipation of the unknown.

Duty replaces reckless abandon and the freedom to express ourselves physically and emotionally.

Over familiarity replaces individuality.

Subconscious and automatic reactions replace presence and alignment to here-and-now experiences as they unfold.

By paying attention to our deepest desires, we tap into our own passion. This is evident when our hearts lift, leap, or swell with excitement when we do something that really inspires us. So whether it is making, creating, listening, watching, or moving, it is the meaningful internal connection that we experience when we connect with something we are passionate about that brings us into a place of heartfelt presence. By giving ourselves this space, we allow a story based on separateness, mutuality, and mystery to unfold. Importantly, by creating a space where we can develop a meaningful inner experience, we do not depend on our partner to provide this for us. In fact, it is from this place of inner connection that we can also regard our partner, for who he or she is, as opposed relating to him or her with a sense of attachment and expectation for who we want him or her to be. Thus, we protect our autonomous nature by regularly taking time out to connect in a wholehearted way with ourselves.

We further protect the intimate and erotic bonds with our partner through consciously creating and staying attuned to boundaries that support us in staying separate and not getting lost in roles.

There's a fierceness and selfishness to desire that needs to be nurtured. Boundaries act to clearly differentiate between different parts of us in the relationship, for example, the responsible one, the caring one, and the playful erotic one. Keeping boundaries in place means that a sense of separation and autonomy can be maintained in this most sensual sphere of the relationship, for example:

We ask for support as opposed to assuming certain roles.

If we do take on certain responsible roles we do so with a sense of balance and measure, whereby other important parts can also be incorporated; including self care, social life, fun, and most of all, a space to connect and re-establish the bonds that brought us together with our partner in the first place.

When we step into roles in our relationship, we sometimes over-serve or become over-dependent. Roles can act to kill desire because when we use up all our resources serving others, we have no space left for our own needs. So when we become absorbed in the roles we undertake where each person does their job to keep the show on the road, such as keeping the mortgage paid and minding the children, there is no novelty or freshness, we become unconscious, no longer present, and suddenly we are not a couple any more.

For a *whole-self-to-whole-self* relationship to develop, we need to create separation so that we can reconnect with ourselves. Novelty comes from the separation and desire is invigorated by it. Therefore, the pathway to desire is created by the space we make to look after and reconnect with ourselves.

As already stated, we each have a need to stay grounded and connected with our inner selves. Therefore, by giving each other space in a relationship, we can breathe and stay centred. This allows us to keep our sense of self intact as opposed to becoming entrapped in our partner's life, and vice versa. Taking time for ourselves affords us the opportunity to keep our focus and sense of purpose in life clearly in our sight in terms of career, social life, and friendships, recreation, and personal time. The consequences when we do not consciously make time for ourselves are:

We easily fall into habits where we over-rely on our partner, taking him or her for granted, and becoming deadened as opposed to enlivened in the relationship.

We do not allow ourselves space to regroup and focus; we cannot be seen in our enlivened state. We are instead seen for what we are not doing and vice versa. We have an idea of what our partner should be doing and who they are, and we think that is the truth.

When we are separate from our partner, we create an opportunity to miss him or her and to imagine what it will be like to be reunited again. This enlivens our imagination and sense of eroticism. By owning our desire, we can sow seeds and allow our partner to fantasize about us.

Therefore, it is vital that we develop our relationship in a way where we regard each other's need for space. In this way, we can create an opening for longing, intimacy, and connection so that the time that we are together can be used in a sensual way. This acts to invigorate the relationship by feeding its erotic energy, so that when we reconnect with our partner, we are able to look at him or her with fresh eyes and experience the attraction all over again.

We are attracted to others when they are enlivened by a sense of purpose or when we see them through someone else's eyes. Similarly, when we engage with other parts of our life with the same sense of purpose that we approach our relationships, we exude a sense of radiance that keeps feelings of attraction and desire alive. This sense of vitality is what enables us to be really seen by each other in a relationship. These feelings have a feedback effect whereby our confidence increases as we experience greater passion and purpose.

However, sometimes we inadvertently and unconsciously stand in the way of nurturing desire and eroticism in our relationships. In some cases, we believe we are protecting our relationship when we take particular actions, when in reality the opposite is the case. I will now illustrate this by bringing into context the very natural transitions that occur in relationships and the behaviours that we adopt in order to adjust to these changes.

Responsibility

As a relationship develops and new responsibilities enter the equation, physical intimacy shifts and the balance that is required to keep sexual equilibrium in place can get lost. This is especially true when children or the financial responsibilities of a mortgage, jobs, etc. enter the relationship. When we fail to keep a balanced approach in our relationship and we instead allow the role of caregiver, provider and/or protector to take over, we unconsciously move into *Mother* or *Father* space and the role templates that were modelled to us in our childhood take over. When we allow this to happen, the quality of the interaction with intimacy and sexual desire can get suffocated. When we take on responsibility for our partner's needs, whether it is to reassure, protect, provide, or satisfy certain expectations, it is very difficult to allow ourselves the freedom to allow our erotic energy to breathe. As a result, our ability to experience freedom becomes stilted and a very meaningful part of us that yearns and longs to be seen becomes overshadowed by a very reactive, protective part that automatically assumes the role of fixer or problem-solver. We unwittingly sacrifice our needs for the sake of the other and consequently, we eliminate any potential for fulfilment in the erotic space of the relationship because erotic energy requires us as individuals to be fully present and alive.

Judgment

When one of the couple lives in a world governed by judgment, any sense of freedom and liberation to act from an unencumbered place of eroticism is stifled. Instead, the yearning and longing for a true and spontaneous connection, physically and emotionally, continues, as part of our self remains unseen. Our erotic energy becomes suffocated by a polarized view of the world, where physical intimacy is governed by ideas and thoughts based on rules, as opposed to mutual connection and caring. Put simply, judgment stifles relationships. When it exists, the relationship operates in a very edited way, where we can only allow certain *acceptable* parts. Consequently, a *whole-self-to-whole-self* connection is compromised, as our full humanity is excluded.

There's also another type of judgment that places a huge obstacle in the way of our own freedom, that is, self-judgment. When our thoughts are clouded by harsh self-judgments such as "I'm not good enough," we cast aspersions on ourselves, while at the same time we compare ourselves to others. When we listen to the voice of our inner critic, we rob ourselves of any chance to experience a true connection. Instead, we act from a place of injured child and ego, where our true self cannot be regarded with honour and compassion. Sometimes, we project our insecurities and shame onto others, often blaming them as a way of coping with our own inhibitions and feelings of inadequacy. Other times we make excuses for ourselves, we joke about ourselves or we judge the other. Consequently, the whole relationship experience is written off before it ever has any opportunity to begin.

Stress

In today's world, we are expected to consistently perform on so many different levels: professionally, intellectually, socially, and physically. We forget that when we experience stress in one area, it is not something that we can suddenly let go of; it is going to affect our private sphere. However, when we only view sexuality as the sexual act, and there is no space for us to be met with presence and consideration in our relationships, physical performance becomes a very real anxiety. We forget that it is the sensual connection we experience with our partner that holds us in the erotic space that the relationship contains. So rather than taking charge and meeting in a mutual space of respect and regard, we fall into the trap of relating to sex as a commodity to satisfy the needs of us, or our partner. We take this a step further when we pile this most visceral sphere of our relationship with expectations, which need to meet some external criteria.

Self-consciousness

When we are self-conscious about our sexuality, we become awkward and afraid to be present and seen by another. Subsequently, the beauty and connection of the experience becomes obstructed, as we cannot meet our partner. When we turn to alcohol to relax our inhibitions, we sometimes take this to an extreme level. When we completely block our inhibitions, we also inadvertently block our ability to remain connected with our emotions and senses. Instead, we meet the other in a disconnected state where only the physical aspects of the union remain present. The erotic experience is just as much sensual and sensory as the sexual experience. We can either meet the other openly from a connected and present place, or we cannot.

The erotic connection we experience with our partner provides the context where we can reconnect through feeling and presence in the most visceral and sensual experience. It switches the focus from functioning in the roles and responsibilities of everyday life such as parent, teacher, carer, or provider, to attention and presence as a partner committed to nurturing the intimate space held between two people in a relationship. These are the human aspects of relationships, which we forget. We so easily get lost in the idealistic context of what a relationship *should* be.

Idealistic expectations are further compounded in this modern and ultra-competitive era, where as human beings, we are being commoditized, constantly evaluated, and expected to perform to consistently high standards, without consideration to our humanity and vulnerability.

In the online environment, the pressure to conform to the ideals of what desirability represents is immense. As this environment of ideals prevails, our perception of ourselves and others is unconsciously shifting from human being to automation. This translates in the sexual arena, where having sex is regarded as a physical need and as a commodity. Accordingly, dating is being asked to take a back seat, as hook ups become the norm, allowing little room for the psychological and emotional aspects of these unions to develop in an organic way. The expectation is that either partner can just show up with little or no consideration to nurturing a sense of ease or reciprocity.

As we fall victim to our own expectations, performance anxiety begins to take hold at work, socially, in relationships, and the sexual sphere. We struggle to be alone and we forget the true art of being with our partner where the simple act of holding or being held with attention and presence can be the most sensual experience of all. This is particularly evident now in a world where Viagra has become a household brand and is widely used. We forget that eroticism has an emotional component to it where it is necessary for us to be emotionally present in order to connect with the other.

When we create sexual bonds on a purely physical level, without any form of emotional, intimate, or spiritual connection, we lose ourselves in a dark and confusing place. We try to escape using alcohol or other dependencies, and in doing so, we numb the vulnerable part of us, which holds the key to our sensuality and radiance. We substitute another form of connection that has no regard for inner feeling and presence.

Most importantly, to experience true desire and eroticism, we need to trust the person we are with, emotionally, physically, and psychologically. Otherwise, we cannot risk letting ourselves go with the unencumbered freedom that is required to enter into and stay in the experience of connection that true eroticism and desire require. When we sense that we are not regarded in the relationship, we begin to lose trust in the bond that keeps us together. A subconscious shift takes place and in an effort to protect ourselves we pull back.

So how do we find our way back to the truly intimate physical space where a relationship truly comes alive, where attunement to emotional, spiritual, psychological, and physical aspects of the relationship can freely emerge, and where the space that the relationship holds becomes enlivened in a profoundly visceral way?

When we step into ourselves and work from the inside out, we can engage with our inner intimate space. What we feel and how we are moved by certain experiences such as our surroundings, a person's voice, their smile, their eyes, how we are held, touched, caressed, the music we listen to, the words we hear, are all experiences that are invoked from places deep within each of us. When we are present in these experiences, the meaning resonates with our very core or coeur, our heart and soul.

When we operate from a place of connection, we tap into our greatest resource, for example:

The wise part of us that knows us better than anyone else.

The nurturing part that wants to take care of us.

The joyful part that wants to experience desire.

The part that loves us with the greatest understanding, kindness, and regard.

When something comes from the heart, it emerges in the most genuine and profound way where we exude a sense of passion and aliveness, desire and sensuality, feeling and longing. We stay connected to this heartfelt place when we nurture and soothe it with spirituality, nature, and compassion.

When we act from a place of presence with ourselves, we recognize and engage with our own sensuality and sexuality. This also signals to our partner that we are truly present. It is this signal that evokes feelings of longing and desire for both. When our partner can meet us here in this place, the experience is one of sexual eroticism and intimacy.

Summary

In order for our relationships to stay alive, we need to move and grow. If we do not allow each other breathing space and the freedom to grow, we suffocate our relationships and the union simply struggles under the pressure of being stifled.

If a relationship is a crucible for growth, as each new layer unfolds, we need to allow room to expand and facilitate the direction of the growth as opposed to becoming cramped and stifled. We need to enable our partner to grow also, ready to adjust to any new direction that the growth heads towards. In a relationship, this can mean two whole beings coming together, growing, meeting again, separating to grow and meeting again.

We feel closest to and really see someone else when they are enlivened by someone or something else. Thus, we never lose sight of intimacy when two whole selves meet and separate, meet and separate, never getting lost in the other.

In order to protect the erotic space of the relationship, we need to allow ourselves the space to nurture our autonomy. This means giving to ourselves the space and opportunity to reconnect with our inner world where we can inhabit our innate energy. Thus, the *Self Centred Approach* asks us to be selfish where we do not become absorbed in the world of our partner and we protect our autonomy by remaining separate. Longing stems from a conceptual "elsewhere" and the notion of reconnection with someone we love. Hence, in order to desire and long for our partner, we need to create space to become separate from him or her. Erotic energy requires this of us, so that when we are reunited with our partner, we invigorate the union with our renewed vitality. Desire and eroticism cannot exist when we become identified by the roles we undertake in the relationship, such as carer or responsible one. In this sensual sphere, we are being asked to connect with our inner world, where we embody our innate energy, from this place we are instinctively drawn to and attract our partner.

When we approach the other aspects of our lives with a true sense of purpose, we become enlivened by the energy that this purpose evokes within us. From this place our partner can see us in our enlivened state, and vice versa. Conversely, when we remain attached to the roles we each play in the relationship, we can only be recognized for the parts that have not been fulfilled; the resultant energy detracts from the erotic energy in the relationship.

Responsibility, judgment, stress, and *self-consciousness* are all the enemies of eroticism and desire. *Responsibility* displaces our own needs as we undertake to fulfil the needs of our partner. *Judgment* replaces our ability to inhabit unencumbered freedom. *Stress* is derived from expectations where we are expected to perform to a physical standard, without consideration to the sensual aspects of intimacy. *Self-consciousness,* along with the methods we use to negate it, creates a barrier to allowing ourselves to truly connect.

We own our sexuality when we connect with the sensual aspects of our life; this requires us to embody the spiritual, psychological, emotional, and physical aspects of our beingness. As we gift ourselves this opportunity, we allow the opening that is necessary to meet and integrate each new mysterious part as it emerges along the pathway to becoming multidimensional, fully present, mysterious beings.

END NOTE

In this book, I have tried to map the pathway to love through first and foremost building a conscious relationship with the self by recognising and holding our unconscious parts when they emerge. We do this when we become curious about our vulnerable feelings in a conscious and compassionate way. By bringing our lost parts into the foreground, we find a way back to our true selves. Moreover, when we enter a relationship with another, we can do so in a mature way where we take responsibility for, and become curious about, our feelings, rather than living from an old script where we experience our hurts in the relationship as something to fear and take flight from.

Most importantly, the relationship space that exists between two people needs air to breathe and space to develop its own mysterious and truly autonomous shape. One of the biggest challenges we face is allowing and honouring this holding energy. I am positing that in allowing and trusting this space, we can open up the pathway for truly profound and often inexplicable feelings and experiences to emerge. We risk interrupting and blocking this emergence when our need for certainty pushes us to try and control; we react by filling silence with words or we ascribe a particular narrative to a story, which has yet to unfold. Other times, we try to be noticed in inauthentic ways.

One of the most important messages I want to deliver is that we do not look to our partner to make us whole, we seek to make ourselves whole, and the relationship provides the crucible for this expansion towards wholeness.

Resentment can provide the surprising opening to connection with our repressed parts because when we experience resentment, we subconsciously recognise in another a very meaningful part of us that we were prohibited from owning at an earlier time in our lives. Therefore, in allowing ourselves to become curious about our reactions, we can consciously open ourselves to recognising, acknowledging, and reintegrating our very meaningful disconnected parts.

This practice supports us in our emergence; it also allows us to deepen our connection with others, as we are no longer blinkered by our resentment.

In a similar way, when feelings of disappointment, loneliness, abandonment, or rejection emerge in our relationships, our automatic reaction is often to blame. However, we have a choice. We can allow these feelings to control how we view ourselves and the other in the relationship, or we can choose a different path where we turn towards our own hearts and we hold, nurture, and heal our very young wounded parts, where these feelings of hurt stem from.

Changing how we perceive the space we inhabit with another takes practice, time, and a commitment to valuing our inner worth. As mentioned throughout this book, it is the connection that we nurture with ourselves where we compassionately acknowledge our journey that ultimately allows us to emerge and be seen. It is also my belief that intimacy can only grow between two people when there is a willingness to grow. We can model intimacy by opening to our partner from a place of true and heartfelt connection with our internal experience. This can be the expression of feelings of love, acknowledgement and understanding, or disappointment, loss, and heartbreak. It is from this place of presence that we invite another heart to connect with ours. However, when we are met with distance, dismissiveness, or defensiveness, we cannot create or belong to an intimate space in this relationship. Rather than reacting to our experience of not being seen or acknowledged, we can allow our conscious selves to adopt a new understanding and compassion towards this other who is unable to meet us with an open heart. Thus, when we choose to occupy a conscious space within ourselves, we can discern and choose relationships where our emergence can be supported and nurtured.

Intrinsic to the approach we take to relationships is our approach to life, where we value who we are and we stay in alignment with our inner purpose. When we act from a place of connection with our heart, we access our courage and we empower ourselves to take risks, where we do not self-doubt, compromise, judge, and blame ourselves, or our partner; and importantly, we do not align our value and worth with the relationship.

It is my belief that we each have a unique star. We can connect with it when we are in tune with our heart. Each time we make decisions and choices based on who we truly are and what our pure intention is, we are in control of our life. Therefore, we choose the direction in which we want to go.

MEDITATION

To support you in connecting with your star, I am leaving you with a meditation, which can be used as a tool to help you connect with your purpose. You may choose to record this meditation—pausing for about fifteen seconds in silence between phrases. You will also need something for jotting down your notes.

Start by sitting quietly and becoming aware of your surroundings . . . Locate yourself in space and time. Feel your back and bottom touching the chair you're sitting in . . . Feel your clothes on your body . . . Hear as many different sounds as you can hear . . . Feel the air in the room . . . Just for now, there's no place you have to go and nothing you have to do . . . Just be here now . . . You can close your eyes if you haven't already done so . . . You can be aware of your breathing . . . Feel the air as it comes in and it goes out . . . Be aware of how it feels in your nostrils as you breathe in and as you breathe out. . .

And now you may be feeling a kind of heaviness in your eyelids . . . You can just let them close tightly . . . You may feel that heaviness in your jaw . . . In your arms and hands . . . You may feel like you can't move your hands . . . And you may feel like there is a heaviness in your legs and feet . . . like you can't move your legs . . . Or you may feel just the opposite, like your whole body is floating . . . like your hands and arms are like feathers . . . You really know what you feel, heaviness or lightness . . . and whatever that is, it is exactly right for you. . .

And now you can begin to step into your future self. Imagine where you are in four years' time. . .

Now visualize where you live . . . Where are you? What are you surrounded by? What does it feel like? Are there particular sounds or images that resonate? Is someone living with you?

Imagine your relationship . . . Can you visualize your partner? How does it feel to be part of this union?

Now imagine yourself . . . You have followed your true passion . . . The trust you placed in yourself means that you achieved your goals . . . You belong to a life that is deeply meaningful . . . Looking back you can see how you simply followed the steps that supported you in reaching this place . . . You provide huge value to others . . . You belong to a community where you are truly regarded . . . You choose to do what is right for you as a person . . . What does it feel like to know this?

Let us move to the time you spend alone away from your work . . . How is this time spent? Are you with others? What are you doing? What are the sounds you hear?

Now take a pen and paper and write down where you can see yourself in four years' time. Write down where you live, what your relationships looks like, what your career looks like, how you spend your time, who is in your life, how you feel.

Next, identify the first steps you need to take to bring you to this place and start putting these steps into action. This is about trusting in your journey and allowing the unfolding that emerges when you are aligned with your inner purpose. You have more than enough to get to where you want to be.

ACKNOWLEDGEMENTS

Firstly, I would like to thank Ethna Sheehan, my mother. Your support has been unwavering. All the little things you do to support me, mean the world to me.

I once heard the saying, "Where you are on your journey is exactly where you are supposed to be". At a time when I reached a crossroads in my life, I met a trusted guide. He listened to me and told me about an incredible course in psychotherapy at Cork Institute of Technology (CIT). There I stepped onto my pathway to becoming a psychotherapist. This has been my gateway to understanding relationships and to honouring my true self. Thanks Maurice O'Sullivan for being my light when I most needed it. Thanks also to the incredible staff at the Department of Counselling and

Psychotherapy at CIT. Your dedication, wisdom, and richness of knowledge never fail to amaze me.

When I wanted to write about relationships, I met Anne Rath, writer and psychotherapist, who encouraged me and remained a steadfast companion on this journey. She opened up a space for me to explore my thoughts and then supported me in translating them to the written word. I hugely appreciate your generosity and support.

I would especially like to thank my friends Mary Fenton and Martin Dunne, who took my final draft and read it inside out and upside down. Importantly, they gave me constructive feedback—something that only true friends can do.

So many great moments have come from the creation of this book. Reconnecting with friends has been one of them. In particular, Ciara Flynn, thank you for the beautiful tree illustration for my front cover (instagram: ciara.flynn.art).

Thanks also to Richard Bradburn @editorial.ie who copy-edited this for me. I hope I did justice to your suggestions. Thanks to Ann Ruth, Deirdre Brennan, Aisling Taylor and Roisín Hickey for your thoughts, opinions and guidance during the creation of this book.

I feel very blessed to have experienced the relationships that I have had. To my companions on the relationship journey, you have enriched my life in a very unique and profound way.

Most importantly, thank you the reader for taking the time to read this. I hope you have found it helpful. I would love to hear your stories. If you would like to connect with me, please go to **www.evieflynn.com**, or join me on Instagram @ evieflynn_ or twitter @evieflynn.

Printed in Great
Britain
by Amazon

31428201R00104